CROWOOD EQUESTRIAN GUIDES

Feeding and Watering

TERESA HOLLANDS

The Crowood Press

First published in 1994 by
The Crowood Press Ltd
Ramsbury, Marlborough
Wiltshire SN8 2HR

This impression 1999

British Library Cataloguing-in-Publication Data

A catalogue record for this book is available from the British Library.

ISBN 1 85223 809 7

Throughout this book, 'he', 'him' and 'his' have been used as
neutral pronouns and as such refer to both males and females.

Dedication

To my mother for all her support, and in memory of my father
before he left the family in 1989.
Also to Karen Bush for her encouragement, Anne Potten and Jean
Bunn (Dengie) for secretarial help, and to the Cuddeford family.

Picture Credits

Photographs are reproduced by kind permission of the following:
Baileys Horse Feeds, pages 21, 56 and 63; Karen Bush, pages 31, 34,
36, 40, 45, 46, 75 (top right and bottom right) and 78;   Dr Derek
Cuddeford, pages 5, 23 and 28; Dengie Crops Ltd, pages 55, 57, 60,
61, 62, 64, 68, 71; Dodson & Horrell, pages 59, 69 and 70;
Horsehage, pages 49 and 91; Redwings Horse Sanctuary, pages 73
and 76; Welsh Agricultural College, page 75 (top left and bottom left).

Line-drawings by Hazel Morgan

Acknowledgements

Typeset by Dorwyn Ltd, Rowlands Castle, Hants
Printed and bound in Great Britain by   WBC Book Manufacturers Ltd.

CONTENTS • 3

Introduction	4	Cereal Straights	58
The Digestive System	6	Other Straights	64
Basic Nutrients	10	Compounds	67
Vitamins and Minerals	12	Feeding Equipment	72
Water	15	The Horse at Grass	74
The Rules of Feeding	18	Herbs and Supplements	82
Feeding Quantities	22	Diseases	85
Standard Diets	29	Summary	92
Special Diets	34	Glossary	94
Problem Feeders	43	Further Reading	95
Forages	47	Index	96

'Man cannot live on bread alone', and although horses and ponies evolved to eat only forages (mainly as grass), the way we keep them, exercise them and alter their natural environment means that they cannot always live on grass alone.

Although horse feeding has been traditionally regarded as an art rather than a science, it is becoming more and more recognized that science plays an important part in feeding horses. However, the practical knowledge of the 'art' of feeding is essential. This can be gained by experience – knowing what a horse likes and dislikes, knowing good-quality feed, and knowing how and when to feed it

This book is intended for people who have not been brought up on the back of a horse, and require a basic understanding of the science – and a guide to the art – of feeding.

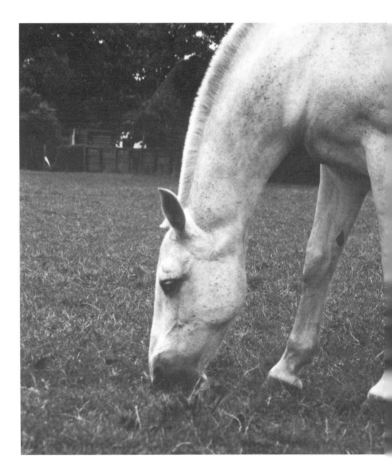

Although grass is the natural feed for horses, a grass diet may need supplementing.

The scientific approach to feeding.

The practical aspect of feeding.

WHY FEED HORSES?

All animals require energy to live. The heart is a muscle which requires a constant supply of energy; cell renewal, growth and general wear and tear all require a supply of energy. It is a well-known fact that horses must be provided with an adequate supply of energy, protein, vitamins and minerals and have access to clean water.

The ways by which we feed our horses and the reasons why we must follow certain rules can only be fully understood by having a knowledge of the horse's digestive system.

The horse has less than an hour to digest and absorb all his feed (except fibre) as it passes through the small intestine.

If you overload the stomach, the food is pushed through the small intestine even faster, which can result in poor digestion and often colic, laminitis or poor performance.

The horse eats large pieces of food which are made up of many chemicals. By physical (chewing), chemical (enzymic) and bacterial breakdown, the horse makes sure that the food is broken into thousands and thousands of small pieces, so small that they can pass through the gut wall into the bloodstream. The minute pieces are then built up again in the body to form proteins, carbohydrates and fats. This whole process is digestion.

Digestion starts in the mouth. Horses have very mobile lips, which they use to select food. They are unique amongst grass-eating animals in that they actually bite and chew the grass before swallowing. A cow will 'rasp' the grass with its tongue and swallow it whole.

A horse will chew a kilogram of hay 3–6,000 times before

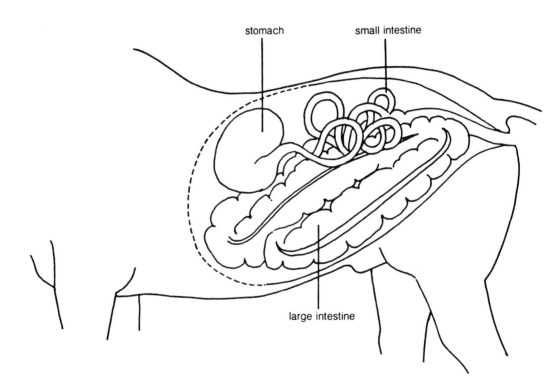

stomach   small intestine

large intestine

Structure of the digestive system
(left side).

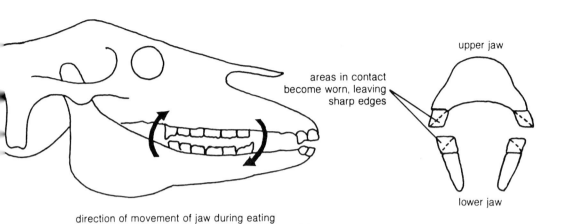

areas in contact become worn, leaving sharp edges

upper jaw

lower jaw

direction of movement of jaw during eating
hooks form where anterior/posterior occlusion is incomplete

Relative positions of the upper and lower jaw; where teeth are in contact during mastication, sharp edges may be formed.

swallowing it, whereas he will chew a kilogram of concentrates only 1,000 times before swallowing it.

A horse produces saliva only when he is actually chewing – his mouth does not water in anticipation of food, so it is important to make sure your horse chews his food as many times as possible.

Horses' saliva does not contain any amylase, a chemical that starts the digestion of starch. Before domestication, the horse's natural diet was low in starch.

Saliva is important because:

- It lubricates the food, thus preventing choking.
- It provides bicarbonate ions (electrolytes).
- It buffers the food as it enters the acid stomach.

Once the food has been chewed to particles as small as 1–2mm, the liquid mass is swallowed and passes down the oesophagus into the stomach.

The horse's stomach is small: it can hold a maximum of only 2.5kg (5lb) of feed in one go. A scoop of feed will swell almost to fill the horse's stomach, once it is diluted with saliva and stomach juices.

Horses have small stomachs because their first means of defence is flight: they have to be able to run from predators and this is done

Always add chaff to hard feed, especially pellets. Horses chew pellets more quickly than coarse mixes.

If you feed too much food in one meal, or feed low-quality feed, you will often see it passing through in the droppings. Food that is too rich can act as a laxative.

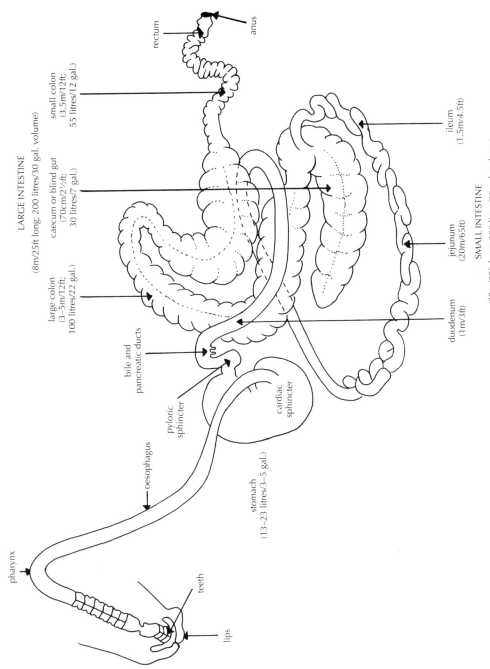

rectum

anus

small colon
(3.5m/12ft;
55 litres/12 gal.)

ileum
(1.5m/4.5ft)

LARGE INTESTINE
(8m/25ft long; 200 litres/30 gal. volume)

caecum or blind gut
(70cm/2½ft;
30 litres/7 gal.)

jejunum
(20m/65ft)

SMALL INTESTINE
(25m/80ft long; 200 litres/30 gal. volume)

large colon
(3–5m/12ft;
100 litres/22 gal.)

duodenum
(1m/3ft)

bile and
pancreatic ducts

pyloric
sphincter

cardiac
sphincter

oesophagus

stomach
(13–23 litres/3–5 gal.)

pharynx

teeth

lips

most effectively if they are not hindered by excess weight caused by a full, heavy stomach.

It is fortunate for us that this is the case: we certainly would not be able to showjump other herbivores such as cows and rhinoceroses!

A small amount of protein is broken down in the stomach and also a little amount of fermentation takes place. Food remains in the stomach for only about twenty minutes, though some foodstuffs will remain for two hours, and are kneaded into a thick liquid mass which then passes into the small intestine.

Here, in the small intestine, the liquid is attacked by different types of chemical to break down chains of molecules to a size small enough to be absorbed through the gut wall into the blood vessels. The chemicals (enzymes):

- Break down carbohydrates (starch) to glucose and simple sugars (the horse is not very good at this though);
- Break down proteins to amino acids;
- Break down fats to fatty acids.

This process has to be completed in less than an hour.

Any food that remains undigested in the small intestine (and this will be mainly fibre), is then passed into the large intestine.

The large intestine is like a very large fermentation vat. It is full of millions and millions of micro-organisms which break down the fibre and use it as a nutrient source. As they break down the fibre, they manufacture B vitamins and release energy, which the horse uses. Food can remain down in the large intestine for up to sixty hours. The horse is primarily a forage eater and spends most of the time digesting the food that he evolved to eat.

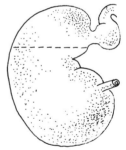

By the time it has been diluted by saliva and stomach juices, a scoop of food will almost half fill the stomach of a 500kg (16hh) horse.

There are ten times the number of micro-organisms in the horse's gut than there are cells in the whole of its body. Changes in feed therefore must be done very slowly, as the organisms need time to adapt.

Any food from which the horse cannot extract goodness is passed out of the body as droppings or urine.

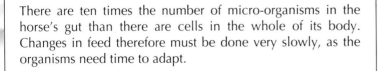

Energy is the most important requirement of any animal. Energy is provided by the three basic nutrients, carbohydrates, proteins and fats. The main energy source fed to horses are the carbohydrates (starch/sugar) which are found mostly in the cereals. A horse is not an efficient digester of starch (sugar) so care must be taken when feeding large quantities.

CARBOHYDRATES

Starch and fibre (cellulose) are made up of glucose. The only difference between starch (cereal sugars) and cellulose (plant sugars) are the links between the sugar molecules. Glucose is needed for muscular activity and for energy for all body functions.

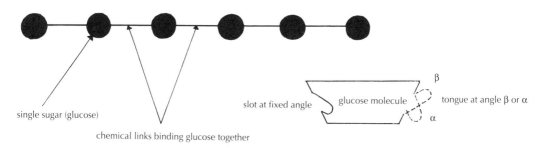

single sugar (glucose)

chemical links binding glucose together

slot at fixed angle   glucose molecule   tongue at angle β or α

β

α

Starch – the main energy source for horses.

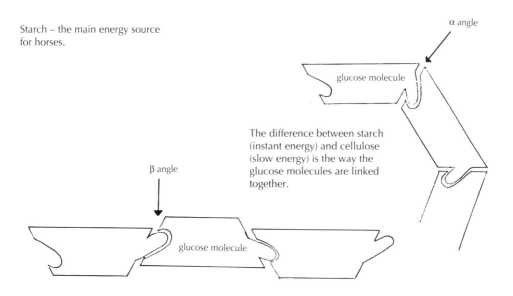

α angle

glucose molecule

The difference between starch (instant energy) and cellulose (slow energy) is the way the glucose molecules are linked together.

β angle

glucose molecule

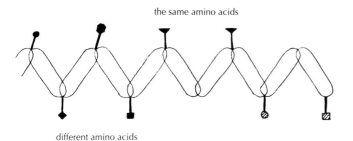

the same amino acids

different amino acids

Proteins are formed in different ways and have different uses within the horse's body.

PROTEINS

These are needed for healthy tissue, cell renewal, milk production and muscle development. They are not a good source of energy. There are about twenty different amino acids in each protein molecule.

FATS

These are another energy source available to the horse. They produce slow-releasing energy like fibre and are less likely to disrupt the digestive system. Fats and oils are made up of different fatty acids and contain two and a half times the energy value of the equivalent weight of carbohydrates.

Lard (animal fat) contains 50 per cent saturated fatty acids and 50 per cent unsaturated fatty acids. Soya oil (vegetable fat) contains 10 per cent saturated fatty acids and 90 per cent unsaturated fatty acids.

Horses are very efficient digesters of fats, but can digest vegetable fats better than animal ones.

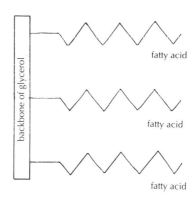

backbone of glycerol

fatty acid

fatty acid

fatty acid

The structure of fats.

VITAMINS

Horses need vitamins in the same way that humans do: they are required in small quantities in the diet for all bodily functions.

Vitamin K and the B vitamins can be manufactured by bacteria in the large intestine if the horse is fed enough forage. Vitamin D is produced by sunlight and Vitamin C is synthesized in the tissues. The table below describes what each vitamin is needed for and how the horse can obtain the vitamin.

VITAMIN	NEEDED FOR	SOURCE
[A]	Night vision. Maintenance of nerves. Correct functioning of the immune system.	Grass. New hay.
[D]	Bone structure. To help absorption of calcium and phosphorous.	Sun-dried forage. Sunlight.
[E]	Muscle integrity. Fat metabolism when it acts as an antioxidant.	Green crops. Cereal germ.
[K]	Blood clotting.	Naturally in the horse's gut. Leafy forage.
[C]	Immunity. Muscle integrity. Antioxidant.	Synthesized in the body from glucose.
B_1 (Thiamine)	Metabolism of carbohydrates, fats.	Naturally synthesized in body. Grains and forage.
B_2 (Riboflavin)	General metabolism. Skin repair.	Synthesized in the gut.

B_{12}	Cell replication. If high levels of concentrates are fed.	Synthesized in gut, requires cobalt.
B_6	Breakdown of carbohydrates, fats and proteins. Formation of haemoglobin.	Synthesized in lower gut.
Folic Acid	Prevention of anaemia, works with B_{12}.	Green legumes.
Biotin	Fat synthesis. Hoof, horn structure.	Maize, yeast, soya bean, green forage.

MINERALS

Minerals are found in small quantities throughout the body: some are important, others less so. The table below summarizes what functions the minerals have within the body.

Minerals	Needed For	Source
Calcium (Ca)	Bone formation. Maintenance of strong, adult bones. Nerve and muscle function.	Alfalfa. Limestone. Milk. Green leafy forage.
Phosphorus (P)	Works with calcium and is needed for the same systems.	Cereals: oats, barley, maize.
Magnesium (Mg)	Maintenance of strong bones and teeth, an electrolyte. Muscle contraction.	Milk. Legumes. Bran. Linseed.

Sodium (Na) Chlorine (Cl) Potassium (K)	Nerve function. Muscle metabolism. Keeping body fluids constant (electrolytes).	Forages. Hay. Grass.

TRACE ELEMENTS

These are required in small quantities compared to minerals, but are nevertheless important.

TRACE ELEMENT	NEEDED FOR	SOURCE
Iron (Fe)	Haemoglobin formation. Enzyme formation.	Most feeds.
Copper (Cu)	Haemoglobin formation. Pigmentation of wool and hair. Cartilage formation.	Herbage. Seeds.
Zinc (Zn)	Healthy skin and hair. Bone formation. Lactation.	Yeast. Bran. Cereal germ.
Manganese (Mn)	Enzyme functioning. Energy metabolism. Fat and protein breakdown.	Forages. Wheat bran.
Cobalt (Co)	Bacteria to make B_{12}.	Pasture.
Iodine (I)	Thyroid gland to work properly. Hormone production.	Seaweed.
Selenium (Se)	Detoxification. Fat metabolism.	Plants.

Water is often forgotten about in the list of necessary nutrients but it is *vital*. Horses should have *clean* fresh water available at *all* times. A horse without water will rapidly stop eating. An 8 per cent deficiency of water will cause sub-acute illness; 15 per cent will cause dehydration and possibly death.

The amount of water a horse drinks will depend upon the moisture content of the feed: grass contains 80 per cent water; compounds and hays contain 12–15 per cent; so a horse on hay will need to drink more water than one eating fresh grass.

> Seventy per cent of an adult horse's weight is water. For example, a 14.2hh pony weighing 400kg (880lb) contains 280kg (615lb) of water; therefore bones, tissues, muscles and fat weigh only 120kg (265lb).

> Resting horses drink 5 litres (1 gallon) per 100kg (220lb) body weight: a 200kg (440lb) pony will drink 10 litres (2 gallons); a 500kg (1,102lb) horse will drink 25 litres (5 gallons).
>
> Exercising horses in hot weather will drink three times more water – 70 litres (15 gallons) – and lactating mares will need two to three times the amount of water required by a resting horse.

- Horses prefer to drink cool, *clean* water.
- Some horses can distinguish various water tastes when travelling from place to place on the show circuit.
- Water troughs and buckets should be cleaned very regularly to prevent souring.

LACK OF WATER

Water deficiency will have a number of effects. It will:

- Reduce feed intake and growth.
- Lead to dehydration which can be dangerous.
- Slow the speed of food through the gut. (Nutrients absorbed from the gut must be in solution.)
- Decrease digestion resulting in colic (from food compaction).

WHEN TO GIVE WATER

Water should always be available: horses may drink before, during or after feeding without interfering with digestion. However, if

Water buckets must be scrubbed daily and refilled with fresh water.

water is not available all the time then offer water before feeding. Do not allow hot, tired horses to drink large volumes of water. Instead, allow the horse to graze or eat damp hay for 30 minutes *or* offer 1–2 litres (1½–3 pints) of water every 15 minutes. After half an hour the horse can be permitted to drink freely.

WATERING EQUIPMENT

A horse at grass should be provided with clean fresh water by means of a trough. However, water troughs should be positioned so that they do not project into the field, or otherwise cause an

(a) wrong

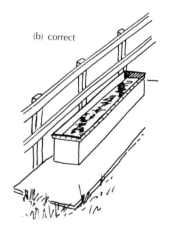

(b) correct

Locating water troughs in the right places is important.

obstruction, as horses may easily sustain injury from them, especially when galloping. For similar reasons, troughs should be inspected regularly to ensure that they have no sharp edges. At the same time, check that the mechanism is functioning properly and remove any debris from the water. Ideally there should be a drainage plug at the bottom so that the trough can be emptied and scrubbed out regularly, otherwise it will be necessary to syphon water out so that cleaning can take place. Always ensure that the ballcock or float mechanism is covered to prevent horses from playing with it. It may be sensible to site the trough on concrete, if possible, in order to prevent poaching.

When the weather is very cold, remember to break the ice on the water troughs. You may need to do this twice a day. Alternatively, provide buckets of hot water and replenish at least twice daily.

In the winter, ice formed in troughs should be broken at least twice a day. If large groups of horses are kept, try to have more than one trough to ensure all horses are able to reach water.

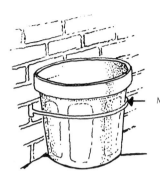

Securing buckets properly to prevent horses from kicking them keeps the bed drier!

Metal ring around bucket

For stabled horses, the two main ways of providing water are with a bucket or with an automatic waterer. If you opt for the bucket, and use it at ground level, you should remove the handles and provide a means of securing it so that it cannot easily be kicked over: one method is to stand the bucket in a car tyre. Buckets should be scrubbed out and replenished daily. A bucket can also be used at shoulder level, secured either with a bracket or in a manger. At this height it is not necessary to remove the handles.

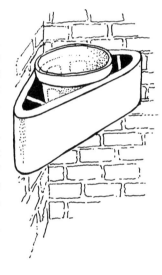

The second method is the automatic waterer. This is a great time-saving device, especially if you are looking after a lot of horses but there are some disadvantages: you cannot monitor the horse's water intake; some horses do not like the noise they make and will refuse to drink from them; and they may become frozen in winter (pipes need to be insulated).

As a general point, you should keep an eye on your horse's water intake: if he is drinking less than usual, find out why.

Automatic waterers are not always the best method of providing water. They can easily become blocked with debris so they need to be checked twice daily.

The rules of feeding really reflect the horse's digestive system so try to imitate as natural a regime as possible. It is important to remember two basic facts: the horse's teeth are designed to eat grass, and the horse has a psychological need to chew. If you follow the rules you are less likely to have problems with your horse, either physically or mentally. Regardless of work load, temperament and type of horse, the guidelines given in this section must be followed.

FEED LITTLE AND OFTEN

The horse's digestive system was designed to have a slow, constant flow of food passing through it. One of the ways of avoiding problems is to feed our horses as they would eat in the wild, where they spend eighteen out of every twenty-four hours eating! This type of feeding is called 'trickle' feeding because there is always a small amount of feed trickling through the gut.

The horse's stomach is very small and it does not have a large storage space for food. A 16hh or 500kg (1,100lb) horse has a stomach the size of a rugby ball. His stomach can hold up to 10 litres (2 gallons), which is equal to a half-filled black bucket of 2½ kg (5lb) capacity, before the food is expanded by saliva and stomach juices. Scale this down to pony size and you can appreciate that the stomach is really very small.

If you overload the stomach, the food is pushed through the gut too fast and is not digested properly. When you overload the stomach, undigested food reaches the large intestine. In the large intestine, there are millions of bacteria which break down the food for the horse. Friendly (useful) bacteria will die as they cannot survive the conditions made by undigested food and the unfriendly (bad) bacteria grow. Poisons are produced which can cause stomach ache (colic), laminitis, swollen legs and other problems.

In order to ensure proper digestion and to avoid overloading the stomach, there are a number of measures you can take:

- Dilute hard feed with lots of chaff
- Feed hay before and after concentrates.
- Feed three to four small meals rather than two larger meals.
- Mix hard feed through hay.
- Feed carrots and apples with hard feed so the horse takes longer to eat.

Keep all containers clean

Just as you would not wish to eat a meal from a plate that had not been washed, horses are similarly repulsed by dirty containers. All containers should be scrubbed daily, otherwise they will become mouldy and slimy and smell nasty. The latter is particularly important to avoid because horses select their food by smell.

FEED LOTS OF ROUGHAGE (FIBRE)

The horse is a herbivore and his digestive system spends the most time digesting the food that is most important to the horse. Food spends up to two days in the large intestine, which is where fibre is digested, and between forty-five and seventy minutes in the small intestine where other food is digested (cereals, for example).

The more roughage a horse gets, the happier the friendly bacteria will be. If he is fed lots of cereals and/or spring grass instead of roughage, the friendly (helpful) bacteria die and the unfriendly (bad) bacteria grow, thus producing poisons which can cause laminitis, poor performance and stomach ache.

To provide adequate roughage, you must feed sufficient rations of hay. However, if your horse is getting 'fat' on hay, feed half the ration as oat straw. Weigh the hay so that you know exactly what the horse is consuming; it might not be enough. Also, feed fibre-based feeds, and bed the horse on straw.

FEED ACCORDING TO WORK LOAD, TEMPERAMENT AND SIZE

Obviously if you provide your horse with more feed (energy) than he requires, he will get fat. Sometimes you do not notice until it is too late and the horse will become slow and sluggish. He will then be suffering from strain on the heart, lungs, legs and muscles.

Alternatively, horses can become over-excited (depending on their character) when fed a lot of food; not a lot of fun and not very safe for the horse or rider.

The best way of monitoring a horse's weight is to measure your horse's heart-girth fortnightly and note it down. You will soon see if his weight is changing.

MAKE NO SUDDEN CHANGES

There are ten times the number of bacteria in the horse's gut than there are cells in the whole of the horse's body. Every time you change the feed (including hay and pasture) not only do the bacteria have to adapt, but so do enzymes. If the changes are quick, many of the helpful bacteria will die and produce poisons that can cause laminitis, colic or at least grumpiness.

One of the commonest reasons for changing the diet suddenly is running out of food, so make sure that you monitor your food supplies so that this never happens. If you decide to alter the diet, it should be done for good reason and implemented gradually over a period of ten to fourteen days. Do not wait until you have run out of the horse's usual feed before buying a different type – whether it is hay or hard feed; instead introduce the new type while still feeding the usual diet.

KEEP TO THE FEEDING ROUTINE

Horses are creatures of habit. They will collect at the field gate when it is feeding time or start banging on stable doors. Fights can occur between groups of horses waiting for their owners to feed them. Therefore, it is extremely important to establish a feeding routine and feed at the same times every day. This means managing time effectively, planning ahead, and if necessary or possible, sharing feed times with other owners so that you can organize a rota.

DO NOT WORK FAST AFTER FEEDING

Exercise causes blood to be diverted away from the digestive system to the heart, lungs and legs. Unless the food has been absorbed before exercise starts, it will not be digested properly.

A full stomach will press on the lungs. If you work the horse fast after feeding, the lungs will not be able to fill with air properly and your horse may not get enough oxygen to his muscles. Also, undigested food will upset the bacteria in the large intestine: some will die, releasing poisons, and stomach ache may occur.

Leave at least two hours between feeding and exercise, and better still exercise first and feed later.

FEED SOMETHING SUCCULENT

Succulents should be sliced lengthways – not in round slices or cubes – so that the horse chews them properly and does not choke.

The best succulent to feed a horse is grass. Grass contains 80–90 per cent water and is the natural feed for a horse. In comparison the food a stabled horse gets – hay and cereals for example – is very dry.

Ideally, turn the horse out daily, but at the least add carrots, apples, sugar beet, dandelions and turnips to the feed every day.

ALWAYS PROVIDE FRESH CLEAN WATER

As pointed out earlier, water is vital for keeping a horse alive. If a horse cannot drink, he will rapidly stop eating.

If he has been deprived of water, he may drink large quantities (a bucket or two). This may wash the food out of the stomach.

Do not worry, however, if your horse drinks a small amount of water during or after his feed.

Each day you should scrub the water bucket out thoroughly; refill with clean water; and make sure it is secure so that horses cannot kick it over.

WEIGH FEEDS AND HAY

You may often find that you are overfeeding because you are feeding by volume *not* weight, so you should weigh foodstuffs regularly to ensure that quantities remain consistent and correct.

Don't forget that pellets weigh more than the same volume of a coarse mix.

The best way of checking food weights is to empty the actual quantity of *everything* you are feeding into separate plastic, non-leakable bags. Take them home and weigh on the kitchen scales. Don't forget to note down the weight.

> A plastic round scoop usually holds:
> 1.3kg (3lb) pellets
> 900g (2lb) coarse mix
> 450g (1lb) chaff
> A slice of hay weighs
> 900–1,300g (2–3lb)

Weigh your hay and feeds to be certain how much you are feeding. Guesswork is inaccurate.

The amount that a horse needs to eat will depend on five main factors: body weight, condition, work load, environment and management and temperament. In order to determine correct quantities you need to take all five factors into account but the most important consideration is your horse's weight.

1. WEIGHT

The table below shows typical weights for certain types of horse, however, as with humans the individual horse may fall either side of the average.

Guide to Average Body weight

Breed	Height		Light		Medium		Heavy	
	cm	hh	kg	lb	kg	lb	kg	lb
Shetland	91.5–122	9–12	160	350	180	400	205	450
Welsh	102–122	10–12	205	450	225	500		600
New Forest	127–142	12.2–14	300	660	320	700	340	750
Thoroughbred Pony	142–147	14–14.2	340	750	360	800	390	850
Arab	142–155	14–15.1	390	850	440	975	500	1,100
Polo Pony	147–155	14.2–15.1	400	880	450	1,000	500	1,100
Hack	150–157	14.3–15.2	400	880	450	1,000	500	1,100
Cob	150–155	14.3–15.1	500	1,100	530	1,175	570	1,250
Racehorse	152–173	15–17	400	880	510	1,125	610	1,350
Middleweight	155–160	15.1–15.3	450	990	470	1,050	500	1,100
Cleveland Bay	152–157	15–15.2	450	990	545	1,200	630	1,400
Heavyweight	157–162	15.2–16	610	1,350	650	1,425	680	1,500
Suffolk Punch	157–168	15.2–16.2	725	1,600	770	1,700	810	1,782
Clydesdale	162–173	16–17	770	1,700	810	1,800	860	1,900
Shire	162–178	16–17.2	900	1,980	OR		MORE	

As with any human weight table, this one is only a guide.

Weighing the horse

There are three methods you can use to weigh your horse. The mos accurate and easiest way is to use a *weigh-bridge*. These are scale specifically designed for horses, but if you do not have access t one take your horse to a local feed mill. In order to use a publi weigh-bridge you will need to take your horse there in a lorry c

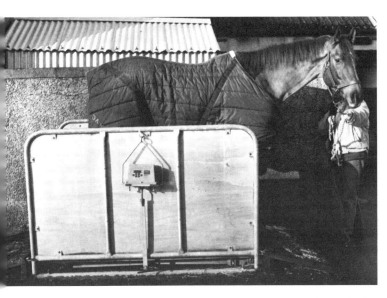

Weigh your horse on a weigh-bridge if at all possible.

trailer. Weigh the vehicle with the horse in, unload and weigh the vehicle without the horse. The difference between the weight of each will give you a fairly accurate reading of the horse's weight.

The second method of weighing a horse is to use a *weigh-tape*, available from all good saddleries. This is a tape that has been calibrated to give an estimation of horse's weight from a heart-girth measurement. Measure the girth just behind the withers and the front legs, pulling the tape tight enough to depress the flesh slightly.

It is also helpful if you keep a weekly record of your horse's waistline in a notebook. You will then be able to detect a change in weight before it becomes visible to the eye.

The third method is to enter your horse's vital statistics into a *formula*. Using a centimetre tape, measure the horse's heart-girth as described above (*see* diagram); then measure the horse's length from his shoulder to his hip. Enter these values into the formula

$$\frac{\text{heart-girth}^2 \times \text{length}}{11900}$$

All measurements should be in centimetres. The number you obtain will be your horse's weight in kilograms.

There is a slightly different version of this equation that you may have seen in other books. Using this formula, the length you

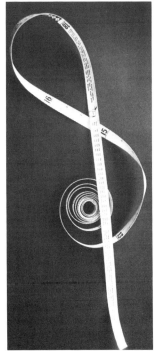

A weigh-tape is fairly accurate: it is likely to be only 5 per cent out. Use a weigh-tape regularly – at least every time your farrier comes.

Using this formula is not as accurate as using a weigh-tape.

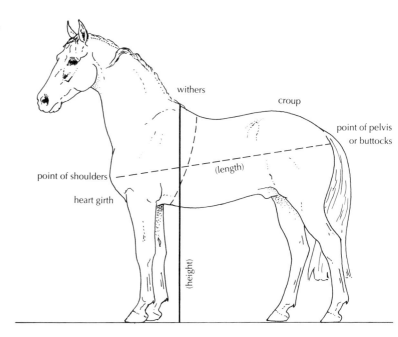

measure is from the point of shoulder to the buttocks and you divide by a slightly different number.

$$\frac{\text{heart-girth}^2 \times \text{length}}{8717}$$

These formulas tend to be inaccurate as errors are introduced when you measure the length of the horse. People tend to obtain slightly different measurements each time they measure, which will affect the answer obtained.

2. CONDITION

As well as 'weighing' your horse you need to take into account his condition, as an overweight horse will need a different diet from an underweight one.

If you are unsure, ask your vet's advice, as other people tend to have a very individual interpretation of what is over- or under weight. However, it should be remembered that a thoroughbred o endurance-type horse will have a longer, leaner look when stood next to a cob.

The following list is a guide to what to look for when assessing your horse's condition:

Very poor   Very sunken rump; deep cavity under tail; skin tight over bones; very prominent backbone and pelvis; marked ewe neck.

Poor   Sunken rump; cavity under tail; ribs easily visible; prominent backbone and croup; ewe neck narrow and slack.

Moderate   Flat rump either side of backbone; ribs just visible; narrow but firm neck; backbone well covered.

Good   Rounded rump; ribs just covered but easily felt; no crest, firm neck.

Fat   Rump well rounded; gutter along back; ribs and pelvis hard to feel.

Very fat   Very bulging rump; deep gutter along back; ribs buried; marked crest; folds and lumps of fat.

3. WORK LOAD

You need to know what work your horse is doing because this will affect his energy requirements. However, the one thing that most horse owners are guilty of is overestimating the work load of their horse.

The following table defines work loads.

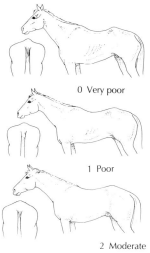

0 Very poor

1 Poor

2 Moderate

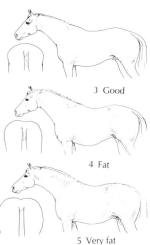

3 Good

4 Fat

5 Very fat

Condition scoring is a useful aid but should not be used on its own.

Work Load	Activity Level
Maintenance	Maintenance of weight, temperature, muscle tone Gentle exercise: moving and playing in the field
Light 1 Light 2	Walking or quiet hacking three or four times a week Some slow cantering and perhaps an occasional show
Medium	Jumping and dressage, probably to affiliated standard Schooling six days a week
Hard	Eventing; cross-country; driving; endurance; hunting
Fast	Racing

4. ENVIRONMENT AND MANAGEMENT

The fourth important consideration when assessing a horse's dietary requirements is the horse's environment. Added to this is the horse's daily management. In order to assess these, ask yourself the following questions in order to establish a picture of your horse's lifestyle

- Is this horse stabled all the time?
- Is he out at grass some of the time?
- Is the grazing good or poor?
- Is the horse rugged in winter?
- Does he stand in a draught?
- Is he kept to a regular routine?
- Is he kept in a busy or quiet yard?

5. TEMPERAMENT

Finally, you need to take your horse's temperament into account. Although this does not have an effect on actual requirements, it will influence the type of feed you want to use. For example, an excitable horse should be fed lots of forage; a lazy horse may need energy feeds such as cereals, *but* bear in mind you cannot feed to change your horse's character.

Using all this information, you can calculate how much to feed your horse. The two factors used to work out quantities are the horse's weight and his work load. The other factors need to be taken into consideration once you have worked out the quantities.

CALCULATING QUANTITIES

Step 1

A horse will normally eat 2½ per cent of his body weight as food irrespective of any other factors. You therefore need to multiply your horse's weight by 0.025; or, if you do not have a calculator handy, multiply your horse's weight by 2.5 and divide the answer by 100.

This will give you the amount of food in kilograms that your horse requires a day. Below are some examples.

Horse Breed	Weight (kg/lb)	Food Needed (kg/lb)
Pony	200/440	5/11
Small Horse	400/880	10/22
Thoroughbred	500/1,100	12.5/27
Heavy Hunter	650/1,430	16.25/36

Step 2

The total daily requirement of food needs to be divided into roughage (hay) and concentrates depending on the horse's work levels. The proportions are shown in the table below.

Work load	Ratio of Hay: Concentrates (per cent)
Maintenance	100 : 0
(Occasionally if hay is of low feed value)	90 : 10
Light Work 1	85 : 15
Light Work 2	80 : 20
Medium Work	75 : 25
Hard Work	50 : 50

For example, a 14.2hh New Forest × Thoroughbred pony weighs 400kg (880lb) and is in light work. The pony is excitable and loses weight easily.

The total amount of food required is calculated by

$$\text{Horse's weight} \times 0.025 = 10\text{kg (22lb)}$$

The horse is in at night and out during the day. Because he is in light work (see table) his feed needs to consist of 85 per cent hay and 15 per cent concentrates. Since he needs 10kg of food altogether, you can work out the actual weight of concentrates required by multiplying 10 by 0.15 (15 per cent).

$$10 \times 0.15 = 1.5\text{kg (3}\tfrac{1}{4}\text{lb)}$$

We do the same for the roughage.

$$10 \times 0.85 = 8.5\text{kg (19lb)}$$

Because he is out during the day we will assume he will eat grass; he will therefore only need half of his roughage as hay.

$$8.5 \div 2 = 4.25\text{kg } (9\frac{1}{2}\text{lb})$$

Computers and the Feedcheck software can be very useful in helping you make accurate changes to your horse's diet.

This is about three or four slices of hay.

It is at this stage that you need to take the other factors into account. For instance, if your horse is overweight, he may not need any concentrates, but a vitamin and mineral supplement instead. If it is very cold, he may need extra hay.

If you are in any doubt then do ask advice. Most horse feed companies employ an equine nutritionist; alternatively you may like to buy your own computer programme, called Feedcheck. More information on these aspects of help can be obtained from your veterinary surgeon.

The table that follows shows the amount of nutrients required by horses in different work situations. Hard work has been omitted as being beyond the scope of this book. The difference in requirements for light 1 and 2 levels is minimal, the only variable being the ratio of hay to concentrates.

Requirements for Working Horses

Weight kg	lb	Work Load	Energy (MJ of DE)	Protein g	Calcium g	Phos- phorus g
Ponies						
200	440	Rest	29	296	8	6
		Light	37	370	11	8
		Medium	46	444	14	10
Horses						
400	880	Rest	54	536	16	11
		Light	71	670	20	15
		Medium	83	804	25	17
500	1,100	Rest	66	656	20	14
		Light	87	820	25	18
		Medium	104	984	30	21
600	1,320	Rest	79	776	24	17
		Light	100	970	30	21
		Medium	121	1,164	36	25

The following pages discuss some practical feeding tips for different classes of horse. Things to look out for and to be aware of are discussed in detail, and an example diet is given at the end of each section.

PONIES

Ponies are usually good doers and it needs to be remembered that many of our native breeds evolved to eat scrubland pasture or sparse mountain grazing. Ideally they would put on condition through the spring/summer in anticipation of winter and gradually lose the weight through the winter. Ponies can generally live on forage alone.

Too often, we feed to maintain or increase weight through the winter, so that once the spring grass comes through, ponies are seriously overweight.

In the spring and summer you may need to restrict grazing:

- Strip graze using electric fencing.
- Beg or borrow sheep (check fencing) and/or cattle to keep grass low.
- Utilize a 'starvation' paddock: quarter to half an acre of poor grazing.
- Top the grass and remove the excess growth.
- Turn the pony out only at night.
- Muzzle the pony for limited periods to reduce, but not stop, his eating, but bear in mind this restricts his ability to drink water!
- If bringing in, then feed oat straw rather than hay.
- Overweight ponies will always be lazy: they need to lose weight *before* you feed them for energy.

In the winter:

- Ponies are better left out, rather than being kept in a stable.
- Ensure the pony has shelter from rain and wind.
- Feed a mix of clean hay and oat straw: put out extra piles to prevent bullying.
- 'Top up' with fibre-based foods if the pony starts to lose too much weight (*see* Types of Feed).
- To prevent poaching do not feed hay near fences, gates or water troughs.

All products fed are slow-releasing 'warming' feeds.

Typical diet for 13.2hh (137cm) pony (250kg)

Work Load
Competing at Pony Club level in the summer, and ridden at weekends in the winter: Light 1.

Feed Required
Body weight × 2½ per cent.
250 × 0.025 = 6.25kg (14lb) of feed
Ratio: 85 per cent hay; 15 per cent concentrates
6.25 × 0.85 = 5.3kg (11½lb) hay + grass + chaff
6.25 × 0.15 = 1kg (2lb) concentrates

Summer	**Exercise/Work**
In during the day	Hacking
Out at night	Working Rallies
	Shows

Morning

Hay-net	1.5kg (3lb) oat straw (2½ slices)
	1.5kg (3lb) hay (2½ slices)

0.5kg (1lb) chaff
0.5kg (1lb) Pasture Nuts or Pasture Mix, or No. 2 Top Line, or feed formulated for horses in light work

If in harder work, substitute 0.5kg (1lb) Country Cubes/Mix or Performance Mix in place of Pasture Nuts

Evening
0.5kg (1lb) chaff as before
0.5kg (1lb) concentrate as before
Turn out: pony will eat about 1.9kg (4lb) dry matter or 9.5kg (21lb) fresh weight of grass.

Winter
Hay on demand, up to ⅓–¼ of a bale, 5kg (10lb) in a day.

Morning	0.5kg (1lb) chaff	
	0.5kg (1lb) fibre-based feed	Pasture Mix meadow-sweet *or* extruded barley plus sugar beet to dampen
Evening	0.5kg (1lb) chaff	
	0.7kg (1½lb) of the product fed in the morning	
	plus sugar beet to dampen	

HORSES IN WORK

You cannot change a horse's character by feeding; so, when first purchasing a horse, you must select one that is conformationally and temperamentally suited to your purpose. However, you must establish a diet that is appropriate for the type of horse and the work he is expected to do. As an example, the requirements of a show/dressage horse, possibly competing in affiliated shows, are described.

THE SHOW/DRESSAGE HORSE

These horses need to be trained to have faultless manners and movement, but must also have a well-conditioned appearance and a shiny coat. However, the most common mistake that people make is to overfeed show ponies. If everyone produced well-muscled rather than overweight animals judges would no longer be able to place fat animals in ribbons.

> Eighty per cent of horses and ponies in the UK are overweight.

Show ponies should be fit and trim, not overweight.

Two nutrients that are especially relevant to the working horse are 'energy' and fibre.

Horses fed too much energy-rich food may behave exuberantly; bucking is frightening, so be careful not to overfeed.

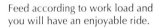

Feed according to work load and you will have an enjoyable ride.

Energy

Energy is needed for working and daily schooling of up to sixty minutes or more, and also to maintain 'a top line'. However, this energy must not make the horse 'fizzy' or 'above the bit'.

Some horses have a reputation for becoming 'fizzy' or 'nervy' when given cereal, especially small quantities of oats. Generally this is caused by excessive cereal intake relative to the amount of work given to the horse. If a horse is not being worked regularly, then the amount of cereal in the ration should be minimal. Cereals (grains) are defined as monocotyledon seeds and include wheat, barley, oats and maize.

Fibre

All horses, no matter how valuable, benefit from being turned out daily. However, many show/dressage horses are stabled, so adequate fibre (hay, chaff, grass, straw) must be fed to the horse. Restricted fibre will result in horses developing boredom habits such as eating their dung, chewing wood, or even windsucking.

You can provide your horse with more fibre and keep him occupied by

1. Extending hard feed by mixing in large quantities of chaff.
2. Leaving a bale of straw in the stable for him to 'play' with and make his own bed. Make sure all baling twine is removed.

Typical diet for a 14.2hh show hunter pony (450kg) or a 15.2hh dressage Thoroughbred (same weight)

Work Load
The horse is being schooled hard six days a week and competed at weekends.

Feed Required
Body weight × 2½ per cent
$450 \times 0.025 = 11.25$kg (25lb)

The horse is in medium work so the ratio is 75 per cent roughage; 25 per cent concentrates.

We will assume the horse is only turned out for exercise, so he requires, per day:

Roughage	Total feed × 0.75	
	11.25×0.75	
	$= 8.4$kg (18½lb)	

This should be provided as 5.5kg (12lb) of hay (4 slices) and 3kg (6½lb) Alfa-A or a forage feed (6 scoops).

Concentrates	Total feed × 0.25	
	11.25×0.25	
	$= 2.8$kg (6lb)	

Examples of concentrates to be fed are Pasture Mix, Top Line Cubes, Country Mix.

If the horse is jumping or eventing then use Microfeed, Racing diet or Performance Mix.

The hay should be split into equal quantities and fed morning and night. The forage feed and concentrates should be split into three equal feeds and 15ml of soya oil added to each feed.

You can use straights such as barley, oats, maize instead of a compound feed, but you will need to add supplements.

Oil
Oil releases energy slowly and has the added benefit of improving coat condition. Feed up to 150ml (¼ pint) a day of soya oil, with a vitamin E supplement, but remember oil provides two and a half times the energy of a similar weight of carbohydrates.

BREEDING MARES

Think very carefully before putting an animal in foal: it is costly, time-consuming and many mistakes can be made. One of the common mistakes is to think that as soon as a mare is in foal, she needs extra food; she does not – at least, not until three months before she is due to foal.

A mare naturally comes into season in the spring and if she conceives, her foal will be born about eleven months later. Obviously 'accidents' do not happen with horses as one has to make arrangements for a mare to be taken to the stallion; however, it sometimes takes more than one go, so the mare may be outside the 'ideal' cycle.

Ideally the mare will conceive in late spring so her foal will be born the following year in time to take advantage of the spring grass.

There are three stages at which feed needs changing:

1. The first eight months

The mare should only be fed as if in light work or for maintenance. From conception to mid-autumn, grazing will normally be sufficient; although obviously if she is losing weight you will need to feed hay and perhaps a small feed. From the middle of autumn through to late winter, a small concentrate feed (low energy food or

Do not breed for sentimental reasons; having a foal requires a lot of commitment.

horse and pony nuts) and ad-lib hay should be fed to maintain weight.

2. Last three months

There is a rapid increase in the size of the foal at this time so the mare should be fed a stud ration plus a high-quality chaff and hay. The mare should be eating between 20 and 30 per cent of her daily ration as a stud mix.

During the last three months of pregnancy a foetus gains 65 per cent of its birth weight, and over 40 per cent of its skeletal structure is developed by the time it is born.

If the grass is lush, then hay need not be fed and the stud ration can be reduced, but a vitamin and mineral supplement must be added.

3. Lactation

This is a very energy-demanding time for the mare and she will require more food now than she did when she was in foal. Do bear in mind, however, that the spring grass is now starting to come through and this is highly nutritious.

If the grass is of good quality, then it is possible that by early summer your mare will no longer need extra feed. Up until then, though, she will probably require 35–50 per cent of her intake as a stud mix. If the grass is not growing well, then additional hay should be fed.

Native Ponies

Native ponies do not require as much feed as Thoroughbreds and it maybe advisable to take advantage of 'concentrated' vitamin and mineral supplements rather than overfeed a stud ration. A fat mare may produce too much milk, resulting in an overweight foal. This could cause serious bone problems later on.

A young foal can gain enough protein and energy from its mother's milk to gain up to 1.5kg (3lb) in weight a day. This intake needs to be correctly balanced with vitamins and minerals. A foal can drink up to 3.75 per cent of its mother's weight a day!

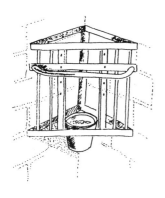

Foals should not be permitted access to their mother's food. A creep-feeder allows the foal to eat its own ration in peace, and has the added advantage that it allows you to monitor intake.

Try to wean the foal when it has the company of other horses that it knows as friends.

Mares and foals should be checked daily.

FOALS

Thoroughbred foals should be fed a creep feed from ten days old; this allows their gut to become accustomed to cereal feed. Natives should also be given a cereal feed for the same reason but only a quarter to a half of the quantity used for Thoroughbreds.

It is advisable *not* to let the foal eat the mother's feed. A foal's intake of hard feed should be monitored and restricted to 450g (1lb) per day per month of age: for example, a two-month-old foal would eat 900g (2lb) of creep feed. If there is a rapid weight increase, then this quantity must be reduced.

Weaning

Weaning is usually done when the foal is six months old; this is normally in the autumn. The foal is put on to a developer ration, quantities will depend upon the quality of grass but normally at least 60 per cent of total feed is fed as concentrates.

Weaning is stressful and if they are not accustomed to eating hard feed, many foals lose their appetite. They start to lose weight until

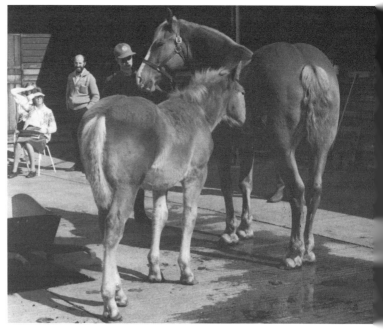

they are used to eating their new feed, and then they overeat. Whenever the growth rate changes, the possibility of developing bone problems increases, so you should aim for a slow steady growth curve.

Growing horses should be turned out for at least twelve hours a day to allow their bones and joints to mature properly. Through the winter weanlings should be fed 1.5 per cent of their body weight as concentrates.

> Native foals may need to be fed less to prevent them from becoming too overweight.

Yearlings

It is best to turn yearlings out on to good grazing after reducing the winter feed slowly. If yours is a native pony beware over-rich grass: *laminitis can occur at any age.*

Come the winter they will require more roughage than they did last year: 50 per cent of their feed should be roughage, 50 per cent should be concentrates. Again, if you are feeding natives this may need to be modified.

Two- to four-year-olds

Generally, you can now treat this age group as though they are mature animals in light work. Hay should be of as good quality as possible and supplemented with concentrates if necessary.

> A 150kg (330lb) weanling needs 2.25kg (5lb) of concentrates (150kg [330lb] × 0.015) and 1.5kg (3lb) of hay. If your young horse is getting fat then this quantity must be reduced.

Feed Intake for young horses

(Note how the concentrate to roughage ratio is different for young horses)

	Age (months)	Forage	percentage of body weight eaten Concentrates
Foal	3	1	1–2 (100)
Weanling	6	0.5–1.0 (25)	1.5–3 (75)
Yearling	12	1.0–1.5 (50)	1.0–1.5 (50)
Two-year-old	24	1.5–2.0 (75)	0.5–1.0 (25)

The figures in brackets represent the percentage of total feed intake constituted by forage and concentrates.

OLD HORSES

Old horses often prove difficult to keep weight on through the winter and will fall away around the withers and the hips. Research indicates that old horses (unlike dogs) have an increased requirement for protein and calcium since their metabolism appears to be less effective at absorbing nutrients.

The practical feeding of old horses often defies science as it appears possible to feed them large quantities of cereals with benefit!

Many old horses have lost teeth and are unable to chew hay well, and some will suffer from colic. Pain and discomfort from arthritis may limit grazing.

Try to follow the guidelines listed below:

> Avoid giving large quantities of hard feed to cold, hungry horses as they may bolt the feed and suffer digestive upsets or even colic.

- Every week, check the condition of your horse (using a weigh-tape and condition score), the pasture value, and the horse's grazing ability.
- Regularly worm and check teeth.
- Provide shelter and protection from wind and rain.
- Rug up in the winter when necessary.

Feed

Dampened pellets mixed with sugar beet are good. If the horse cannot eat hay, then use forage pellets mixed through with high-quality chaff. Feed a specific mix when available or a stud mix; both of these should contain high-quality protein and a good array of vitamins and minerals. Boiled barley or damp cereal mixes are easier to chew than pellets, and hay can be softened by wrapping it in damp hessian for a couple of hours before feeding. Garlic, cider vinegar, cod liver oil and possibly herbs help arthritis, if your horse suffers from this.

If possible, you should also see that your horse has some gentle exercise, rather than spending all his time resting.

None of these tips will keep your horse going forever. Sometimes you just have to know when to let them go.

Hay is one of the most 'warming' foods you can give to a horse.

> Horses over four years old cannot digest milk powder.

Daily feed required for 14.2hh (144cm) Welsh × Arab

Summer
Grazing with perhaps 0.9kg (2lb) forage feed or pellet.

Winter
Forage
As much hay as he can eat or
4kg (8lb) low-molasses chaff
1.5kg (3lb) dampened pellets (grass/alfalfa/hi-fibre/pasture)
1.5kg (3lb) (dry weight) sugar beet (soaked)
Mix the 7kg (16lb) of feed together and use as a hay-net

Concentrates
Up to 3kg (6lb) (possibly dampened) of stud/veteran/extruded mix per day mixed with a small amount of chaff.

COLD WEATHER

Adult resting horses, who are ridden only at weekends in the winter, are best supplemented with roughage (good-quality) hay during cold spells.

Do not be deceived into thinking that boiled barley or hot mashes will warm a horse (although it might make you feel better!)

Fibre is the most warming feed that you can give a horse.

Feed plenty of chaff and fibre to your horse through the winter.

Cereals, pellets and coarse mixes are broken down fairly rapidly and digested in the small intestine. Because the breakdown is quick and easy it requires very little energy and releases very little heat.

Fibre, however, takes a long time to digest. The bacteria have to exert energy to break down the fibre, and in doing so they produce a lot of heat. This heat has an internal warming effect for the horse. The fibre is, in fact, being fermented and the heat released is similar to the heat released during wine- or beer-making; ironically, the best 'top-up' to forage are those mixes described as 'non-heating', which are generally relatively high in fibre.

If the weather is very cold, then additional cereals may be required. Remember to site feed bins and hay-nets away from the wind in sheltered areas in the field.

POOR CONDITION

If a horse is in poor condition it usually has a dull coat and bad feet. There are four main reasons why a horse may be in such a state:

1. Neglect – the horse is not being fed enough for his work load or maintenance.
2. Worm burden; if you think your horse has worms, speak to your vet for advice on an appropriate programme and have a worm count done on the droppings. Sometimes a blood test is necessary.
3. Bad teeth, either with sharp edges or none at all! An annual check by an equine dentist is vital.
4. Quality of feed: check the ingredients in feed and the energy content. Confirm that consistent ingredients are being used. Use a reputable brand from an appropriate manufacturer. If a manufacturer is not prepared to send you written confirmation of what is in the feed do not use it.

Poor foot growth

Many horses develop hoof cracks or sand cracks during either very dry or very wet conditions. Often this is caused by dehydration of the hoof wall. Dampening the hoof and then sealing the moisture in with a hoof cream or animal fat will help this condition. Ask your farrier to recommend a hoof cream.

Supplements containing calcium, lysine, methionine (protein), zinc and biotin (all need to be included) will promote better hoof growth.

Correct feeding and proper care will ensure good feet.

Regular visits by the farrier will help keep your horse's feet in good condition.

Those supplements based on alfalfa often have the most positive effect. Research by Dr Sue Kempson at Edinburgh University showed positive results when alfalfa and alfalfa-based supplements were fed to horses.

Poor coat

This may be caused by the same deficiency that resulted in poor foot growth. Coat condition is often a reflection of diet.

An elderly horse who appears to have a winter coat all-year round may be suffering from Cushings Disease (*see* page 89).

If your horse is on a predominantly roughage-based diet, he may be lacking oil: add two to three tablespoons of soya oil to a small feed of chaff daily. Many feed manufacturers market soya oil and it is cheaper buying it from them than in the supermarket!

OVERWEIGHT HORSES

Eighty per cent of the horses in the UK are overweight and many of them are found in the show ring! Obesity can, however, be a genuine problem in good doers and greedy horses. A mixture of restricting food intake *and* regular exercise should be used to control weight. Try implementing the measures below.

Sand paddocks make useful exercise and turn-out areas for overweight horses.

1. Turn out on limited grazing or sand schools twenty-four hours a day. A horse is more likely to move around and therefore use more energy outside than if kept in.
2. If in a sand school, then feed oat straw or mature cut hay of low feed value; make sure you get it analysed first, however.
3. Gentle exercise twice a day is necessary; try walking out, gentle lunging or even trudging behind a cart.
4. If you are only able to turn him out on good grass, then muzzle during the day to restrict but not stop intake; but bear in mind horses cannot drink so well when muzzled.
5. Provide adequate shelter but do not rug so warmly. Horses can use up quite a lot of energy keeping warm!
6. Feed a vitamin/mineral supplement but no 'hard feed'.

Slow weight loss is likely to be effective; do *not* starve a horse.

NERVY/FIZZY HORSES

Some horses that are quiet and well mannered at home may appear to change their temperament at shows. Nervous horses can lather up, sweat, get fidgety and stroppy to handle; some develop a runny cow-pat scour and seem to undergo a complete character change. (Some of these symptoms are also mirrored in their human counterparts!)

Breeding and immaturity can be contributing factors (as with, for instance, Thoroughbreds); and the unfamiliar surroundings and show day noises can increase fizzy behaviour. In many cases re-schooling of both horse and rider, coupled with increased experience of show days, can help. However, a lot of the problem is overfeeding energy foods for the work in hand, particularly to stabled horses that are not turned out for a *minimum* of two hours a day. Ideally these types of horse will benefit from being fed more food that releases energy slowly rather than quickly.

People often make the mistake of misjudging their horse's work load, assuming it to be harder than it is.

Recent research has suggested that the starch (sugar) from certain cereals, such as oats, is digested more quickly than other cereals. The energy is available to the horse within about two hours of being fed, which is often about the time we leave before riding them!

Thoroughbreds do not control the metabolism of sugar (starch) as efficiently as other breeds and their blood sugar levels will stay high for up to three or four hours after being fed, so that instant energy is available to them just as we are about to ride them.

These types of horse need to be fed:

All horses – even those in very hard work – benefit from being turned out daily. Rug up if necessary.

- Lots of roughage.
- Small concentrate feeds diluted with fibre feeds to slow down their eating and to reduce the rapid release of energy.
- Oil as an energy replacement for some of the starch-rich cereals.
- Grass: that is, they should be turned out daily come rain or shine.
- Low-energy rather than high-energy feeds.
- Also perhaps a yeast or herbal supplement.

Tip: Fats and oils take more time to digest and release their energy than do carbohydrates.

FUSSY FEEDER

Some horses, no matter what we feed them, seem finicky and will not eat enough food to meet their requirements. The causes for this

Example Ration using mainly slow-releasing energy sources 15.1hh (153cm) Thoroughbred Mare (450kg)

Work Load
Ridden daily, showjumping/dressage unaffiliated competitions at weekends: Light 2

Feed Required
Body weight × 2½ per cent
450 × 0.025 = 11.25kg (25lb) of feed
Ratio: 80 per cent forage; 20 per cent concentrates

Forage per day
11.25 × 0.8 = 9kg (20lb)

Concentrates per day
11.25 × 0.2 = 2.25kg (5lb)

Summer
Most *forage* requirements will be provided by grass as the horse should be out as much as possible, as long as there is not rapid weight increase. If in at night then 2.7kg (6lb) or 2 slices of hay should be fed.

Concentrates
1.5kg (3lb) (3 scoops) alfalfa chaff
(if keeping weight on then use a lower feed-value chaff).
0.5kg (1lb) fibrous mix, e.g. Pasture Mix, meadow-sweet
0.25kg (¼ litre) soya oil
Yeast and/or herbal supplement.

Winter
Out at grass 4–6 hours per day; rugged up.

Forage per day
7kg (16lb) hay
2kg (4lb) alfalfa chaff

Concentrates per day
0.5kg (1lb) dry weight, then soaked, sugar beet
2kg (4lb) high-oil/high-fibre mix or extruded feed
0.25kg (¼ litre) soya oil

are many and varied and include sickness, unpalatable, poor-quality feeds, ill health, pain, fever, mouth conditions (especially sharp teeth), sudden changes in feed, distracting surroundings, lack of roughage in the diet and hard work.

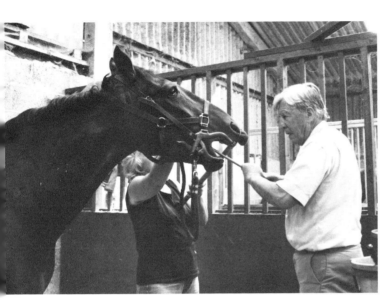

Make sure that *all* your horse's teeth are checked regularly: ensure that your vet does more than just a quick rasp. The importance of good dental care cannot be over-emphasized.

Teeth problems can cause either refusal of food or inability to put on weight. Signs of teeth problems include picky eating, quidding, dropping food from mouth, not being able to eat hay easily or very slow eating. Get your horse's teeth checked *at least* annually by a reputable equine dentist; young and old horses are those most likely to have problems.

Sudden changes in feed (lack of roughage)

The horse is predominantly a forage eater and has literally billions and billions of bacteria in his gut. The bacteria are there to digest roughage, so if there is not enough roughage, or if you change feed rapidly, many bacteria die. This totally upsets the digestive system, giving the horse almost permanent indigestion.

Unpalatable Food

Horses are strange creatures and have definite likes and dislikes – some horses will not touch polo mints! They do not like dusty or mouldy feedstuffs. As horses distinguish their feed by smell they sometimes refuse to eat if they cannot smell, if they have a cold, for example.

Make any changes of feed (including supplements) slowly over at

Disguise supplements in honey: he might like the sweet taste enough to lick it off the spoon!

If one owner regularly rides late, ask him to feed your horse when he leaves, so the horse eats in relative peace and quiet.

Boredom
Horses stabled twenty-two hours out of twenty-four often go off their feed because of sheer boredom. All horses benefit from being turned out, even when they are exercised hard.

least ten to fourteen days. If horses will not eat supplements you can:

1. Make a jam sandwich, mixing the supplement with jam and putting it between bread.
2. Put the supplement in the middle of an apple.
3. Mix it into a watery paste and use an old worming syringe to administer it.

Do not feed old, prickly hay that is full of stems: most horses find this unpalatable.

Noisy or isolated surroundings

Nervous horses are often easily distracted by noisy surroundings, especially at feed times. Some Thoroughbred types may never settle in a busy DIY yard when feeding times are not synchronized or when owners are often still riding horses at 9.00 at night!

If the horse is distracted then a manger over the door rather than at the back of the stable may be more appropriate, as the horse can then eat and watch rather than rushing backwards and forwards constantly.

Lack of company may also reduce appetite; horses are after all herd animals. If you cannot afford another equine companion, what about a goat?

Solution: reduce the bulk

Feed dense, energy-giving feeds to entice your horse to eat. For example:

● Replace straw chaff with alfalfa chaff.
● Replace conventional oats with naked oats.
● Replace 2kg (4lb) of a pasture mix with 1kg (2lb) of competition mix.
● Use oil or fat as part of the energy ration. Oil contains two and a half times the amount of energy contained in a similar weight of carbohydrate.
● Use highly digestible rather than poor quality forage.
● Mix in succulents such as carrots, apples, sugar beet.
● Feed small, regular feeds and do not over-face the horse.

GRASS

The value of grass to a horse depends on how much is eaten, its chemical composition and how available the nutrition in the grass is.

Grass contains carbohydrates, proteins, vitamins and minerals and water, and young grass can provide all the nutrition a horse needs. Young grass contains water (85 per cent), highly digestible nutrients, soluble carbohydrates (starch and sugars), a high amount of protein and a small amount of fibre. As grass matures, it becomes progressively less nutritious.

Sugars

The level of sugars in grass varies between types, as the table below shows.

Grass Type	Water-Soluble Carbohydrates (sugar) (g per kg of fresh grass)
Italian ryegrass	48
Perennial ryegrass	38
Cock's-foot/timothy	22
Red clover	20
Alfalfa	16

Too much water-soluble carbohydrate (sugar) can cause laminitis.

The sugar content of grass also varies with the time of day and the seasons: sugars are lower in the grass in the morning, increasing through the day, and are much lower in autumn than in spring.

Protein

The protein content of grass can vary from 5 per cent in mature grass to 25 per cent (DM) in young grass, and the leaves contain more protein than the stem. However, the protein content of grass can be increased in direct proportion to the amount of nitrogen fertilizer applied to it, so bear this in mind if you are feeding grass pellets!

The protein content of perennial ryegrass, relative to age.				
	Stage in grass development			
Protein	*Cut 1*	*Cut 2*	*Cut 3*	*Cut 4*
g/kg on an as-fed basis	33.4	30.6	30.36	24.25
percentage of protein in grass	3.3	3.0	3.0	2.4

Fibre

Fibre is found in the cell walls of grass. There are different types of fibre: cellulose, hemicellulose, lignin and silica. The nutritional value of the forage depends on how much of each of these is found in the grass.

Cellulose is found in larger quantities in young grass, and can be digested by the horse using bacteria in his lower gut. Hemicellulose increases as the grass gets older; because the horse cannot digest this very well, he can get fewer nutrients out of the grass.

Lignin appears once the grass has grown tall and has started to

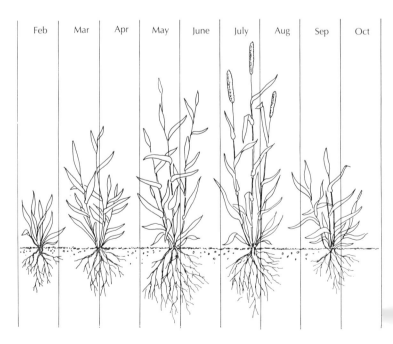

| Feb | Mar | Apr | May | June | July | Aug | Sep | Oct |

How grass grows in a year. We cut hay in the height of summer when grass is not so nutritious and is high in lignin.

seed and flower. It supports the grass (or hay). Not only can the horse not digest lignin at all, it sometimes prevents him from digesting other nutrients in the grass so well.

As the grass gets more mature, its feed value is considerably less. This is why supplementary feeding is needed through the winter, but not necessarily through spring and early summer.

Minerals and vitamins

Grass leaves contain more calcium, magnesium, sulphur, molybdenum and iron than stems. Deficiencies of certain minerals are usually linked to a soil type, although using unbalanced fertilizers could also be a cause.

The practical feeding of grass is described in 'The Horse at Grass'.

HAY

Hay is dried, preserved grass. Generally, grass is cut when it is mature in order to provide as many tonnes per acre as possible; unfortunately, this is when it is at its lowest nutritive value.

When making hay the aim is to dry the grass so that the moisture content can no longer support plant and microbial enzyme activity. The hay should only be 15–20 per cent moisture.

Hay making. Good hay is difficult to make in the UK because of the shortage of good drying days.

Hay feed value will vary and depends upon where and how well it was harvested. If you are buying hay in advance, it is advisable to buy it from one source only. Obviously hay grown and harvested in different areas will vary in nutritional value. The horse's gut needs time to adapt to these changes in the same way it needs time to adapt to cereals and hard feed.

From grass to hay

When grass is dried to make hay, oxidation occurs; this is seen as colour loss. The drying process also causes changes in the nutritional value of grass, although the extent of these changes will vary according to the weather. Rain will leach soluble minerals, sugars and proteins from grass drying in the field. Plant enzymes use moisture to break down soluble carbohydrates and proteins in grass, so the longer it takes to dry, the greater the effect of the plant enzymes, and the greater the nutritional losses. There is also a reduction in vitamin content. For example, the vitamin A precursor Carotene (which is also found in carrots), can be reduced from 100–200mg per kg DM to 2–20mg per kg DM, depending on the length of time that the grass takes to dry.

Mould   Mould is most likely to occur in hay that has taken a long time to dry, so hay that has been produced during a wet summer is far more likely to contain mould than hay that is produced in good drying conditions.

Mould spores present in hay and straw are a common cause of respiratory problems in horses. If you find the slightest signs of mould in hay, do not be tempted to feed it to your horse: even hay that has only a few mould spots on it can cause serious problems, especially in horses that are particularly susceptible to respiratory disease.

Mould spores are visible as the clouds of dust that are typically produced when poor-quality hay is shaken. Such hay can be improved by soaking it for twelve hours before feeding, although horses that are known to be sensitive to mould spores should not be fed hay at all. Such horses are better fed on ensiled hay, or haylage.

Storage   Hay should always be stored in cool, dry conditions. If the hay has not been completely dried before storing, losses of food value will continue; if the hay becomes hot, the proteins present in hay will change structure and become unavailable to the horse.

Hay Analysis

If you buy hay in bulk, it is worth getting it analysed. Whilst two samples may look identical, one may contain 6 per cent more protein than the other: such a discrepancy will influence the amount of hard feed you need to give in order to achieve balance. This is important because it can quite easily result in over- or under-feeding.

How to feed hay

Using a Hay-Net   This is the traditional method of feeding hay and has the advantage of being human orientated: they can be made up prior to using, they keep the floor of the stable tidier, and generate less waste. The horse also takes time to pull hay out of net, which means he is less likely to gobble his food down or eat too much.

You have to bear in mind, however, that the horse is not a giraffe! The hay-net puts his head in an unnatural position, which could be uncomfortable for him. Some horses can untie them. Some owners do not tie them high enough, so once they are empty they drop and there is a risk of the horse putting his feet through the net.

Furthermore, the horse is putting his nose right in the middle of the hay where he is most likely to breathe in spores and dust, which could give him respiratory problems.

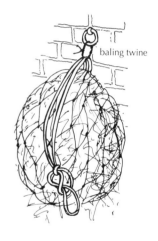

baling twine

Hay-nets prevent mess.

Good Hay
1. The colour should be green to pale fawn – the greener it is the better.
2. It should smell pleasant, not musty or of mice, but not too sweet either.
3. When you shake it, it should not stick together and it should not be dusty nor make you cough.
4. There must be no trace of mould or damp. You will need to open a bale to check this.
5. It should be free of too many weeds such as docks, nettles and thistles.
6. It should not be too stalky.

Feeding on the Floor or Ground   This is a quicker and more natural method, and is also less dangerous for the horse as there is nothing for him to get entangled in. If you shake hay out in field, it will also reduce coughing problems.

The disadvantages of this arrangement are that it is usually messy and can be rather wasteful.

Making a manger

Making a corner manger at floor level is not difficult. Simply partition off a corner of the stable by putting runners down the walls and slipping a piece of hardboard down in them to make a triangle.

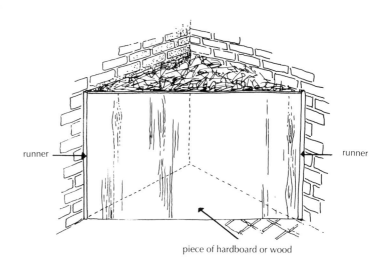

runner   runner

piece of hardboard or wood

Feeding hay at ground level is more natural for the horse.

This is obviously a less untidy and wasteful method than simply strewing the hay on the floor, and is more comfortable for the horse to use as well. You do have to remove the partition weekly, however, to sweep the floor and remove any collected debris.

Weighing Hay
Weigh your hay once a week so that you know how much you are feeding. A bale of hay weighs approximately 25kg (52lb). A wad or slice generally weighs 1–2kg (2–4lb).

Hay must be totally submerged for effective soaking. Use a large weight to ensure that it remains submerged.

If the bucket is not large enough, it will be necessary to turn the hay to make sure that the top half is as thoroughly soaked as the bottom.

Soaking hay

Before hay is fed to the horse, it should be soaked for at least half to one hour. For this you need a large water butt or other watertight receptacle that is large enough to allow the hay to be completely submerged.

The hay should be wet when fed to the horse, so if it has dried after a previous soaking, it will need to be soaked again. Since hay will lose some of its nutrients into water, it is preferable to try to avoid repeated soakings and instead to soak once, and thoroughly, before feeding it.

It is very important to use clean water for every batch of hay to be soaked. Water used for hay soaking will be contaminated; the biological value of such contaminated water will be a hundred times that of raw human sewage, so at the end of each soaking the water should be discarded and the butt emptied and cleaned before being refilled.

Important
Make sure you remove all baling twine before feeding hay. A pair of scissors and a sack in which to put discarded twine should be kept in the hay store.

HAY ALTERNATIVES

Haylage

This is a cross between hay and silage. It is preserved grass which is cut at the same stage of growth as hay, so it could be equally low in feed value; check this with the manufacturer. Instead of being dried to 20 per cent moisture, however, it is dried to only 50 per cent. It is then vacuum packed and 'pickled' in its own juices to preserve it.

Because it has not been allowed to dry for as long as hay it will not have lost so much nutritional value and will usually be similar to the mature grass in feed value.

The 'pickling' of the grass also means it is dust-free, making it a particularly suitable feed for horses sensitive to mould spores in the atmosphere.

Disadvantages   Haylage is dust-free, convenient, clean and easy to handle. However, it does have disadvantages:

Bulk
Straw can be mixed with hay to give the horse more bulk without increasing the nutritional value too much. It can also be used to bulk out haylages.

1. It is expensive (although so is the vet if you have to call him out when your horse contracts a respiratory illness from mouldy hay).
2. It needs to be used within three to four days of being opened and exposed to the oxygen in the atmosphere.
3. Horses tend to eat it quickly as they enjoy it so much, so they may be left without roughage for several hours. Feeding in a small-hole hay-net could solve the problem.

Big bale haylage

This is ideal for big yards or if you have more than five horses. It is made in the same way as small bale haylage but an inoculant is added. This is extra bacteria similar to that found naturally on the grass and ensures that all of the big bale is fermented equally.

Big bale haylage needs special handling equipment, but can be positioned in the fields before it gets muddy. The bales are then opened as required, which helps prevent poaching along the fences.

Short-chop forages

These are a useful hay alternative, as long as they do not contain high levels of molasses and the length of chop is at least 2.5cm (1in). Research work has shown that the rate of passage of short-chop forage through the horse's gut is virtually identical to that of longer-length hay.

The advantages are that short-chop forage does not deteriorate once opened and can be kept for six months if it is stored in dry conditions, out of direct sunlight; it has a known nutritional value, and is, like haylage, clean, dust-free and easy to handle.

However, like haylage, it is also expensive and cannot be fed in a hay-net. It is best fed in a deep corner manger or on the floor in the corner of the stable as previously described.

This type of product can also be used to 'extend' hard feed. The horse will then take longer to eat his cereals, he will trickle feed his hard feed and start on his hay later. Therefore the hay will last longer.

Short-chop forage is extremely useful as a hay replacer or extender.

Straw

Straw is the stalk left after the cereals have been harvested. It has the same feed value as hay that has been grown for seed, that is, all the parts that are high in nutrition have been removed, leaving just the fibre. Because the leaves and seeds have been removed, there is little dust associated with straw unless it has been dried badly.

Straw is a serious alternative to poor-quality hay and can be used as a valuable source of forage, particularly for laminitic ponies. Oat straw is best, but if you cannot obtain it then barley straw can be fed instead. Do not use wheat straw as this is more lignified so the horse will not be able to digest it very well.

Supplementing forage

Most preserved forages are low in vitamins and minerals. Some hays and all straws are low in protein, so unless your horse is overweight you will probably need to supplement with a compound feed. It is best to use feeds that are high in fibre such as high-fibre cubes, forage feeds or low-energy coarse mixes that are high in fibre. These will be digested in a similar manner to the straw or low-quality hay. Alternatively, you can feed a general vitamin and mineral supplement with a handful of chaff.

Straw Chaffs   There are numerous straw or hay (or a mixture of the two) chaffs on the market. They are generally mixed with a high

Useful for bulking out feeds, some people are concerned about the high molasses content of high-calorie chaff.

Pellets will be eaten much faster than chop; the volumes are the same but the weights are different.

> The horse has a psychological need to chew and powdered fibre in pellets and cubes does not give him that opportunity.

> Mix high fibre/forage pellets through straw or hay of low nutritional value to increase feed value and to provide vitamins and minerals. If you have to use pellets and no hay, then feed hourly and mix with lots of chaff.

percentage (sometimes as much as 40 per cent) of molasses or a similar product to improve nutrition and palatability. Some have additional herbs or vitamins and minerals added.

They are a useful source of bulk, ideal for ponies who do not really need any feeding but need to be kept occupied whilst others are being fed. However, except for the molasses, which is high in energy, they are no more nutritious than the raw materials from which they are made. There has been little or no research done on the effect of a high intake of molasses (which is a sugar derivative) on horse's teeth.

The fibre in them has generally been chopped very fine and you should not consider them as hay replacers. They are most useful for mixing with concentrates or hard feed in the bucket.

High-Fibre Pellets and Complete Cubes   These are pellets that are made up of ingredients that are generally low in energy but high in fibre. If you read the label on the bag, you will find ingredients such as rich pollard (bran), NIS (nutritionally improved straw), grass meal, cereal fibre meal (oat, barley and wheat 'middlings', which are the fibrous part of the cereal and not the grain itself).

It is not advisable to use high-fibre cubes as a complete hay replacer, but rather as a hay or forage supplement. The fibre in the pellets has been ground to powder, which the horse can chew very easily, and in some cases he will bolt the pellets. Horses should be able to trickle feed, and they cannot do so easily with pelleted fibre. High fibre or complete pellets are used 'successfully' in Germany; however, Germany also has a high incidence of colic!

ALFALFA

Alfalfa is a legume and comes from the same family as clover, peas and beans. It is the most extensive forage grown throughout the world and is fed to more animals than any other form of forage.

It can be used either as a straight or as a 'forage feed'. Rather than just the seed being harvested as in cereals, the goodness of the whole plant is used, so the end product is a forage.

Alfalfa can be fed as hay (sun or barn dried), as a short-chop chaff (high-temperature dried) or in pellets (usually high-temperature dried).

Unlike most roughages, alfalfa has a high feed value. It is an excellent source of protein as well as providing valuable fibre, calcium and other minerals. In the short-chop form, it is an excellent fibre source for horses suffering from COPD as all dust has been extracted. Alfalfa hay tends to be dusty but despite this is commonly fed to racehorses.

Alfalfa differs from cereals in that it is high in protein, but low in energy, while cereals that are high in protein are often high in energy. Alfalfa contains very low levels of soluble carbohydrates when compared to cereals and this is one of the main reasons that it is successfully fed to laminitic ponies and horses.

Alfalfa really falls into a category between straights and compound feeds; it is a forage feed.

> Alfalfa is marketed in the UK as 15 per cent protein but it is low in energy. High protein does *not* mean high energy. Maize is one of the highest in energy out of all cereals and also one of the lowest in protein.

The main reason that cereals and compound feeds are fed is to counter-balance the nutritional deficiencies in hay. Alfalfa has a feed value similar to concentrates, so you can reduce your reliance on cereals; this is better for the horse's gut.

Alfalfa has become accepted in the UK as a beneficial, staple part of a horse's diet, much as oats have been for years.

> Alfalfa is lower in energy than oats, but is high in calcium, protein and fibre.

Horses that are working hard or horses that require more energy than can be obtained from forages and forage feeds will need to have their diet supplemented with energy feeds. If energy feeds were unavailable there would be numerous activities that we would be unable to do with our horses; for example, showing, jumping, and feeding old horses, young horses and broodmares. We need to supplement forage because we have changed our horse's natural lifestyle.

Energy feeds are mainly cereal feeds, which can either be bought and fed as individual ingredients (straights) or mixed together and bought as compounds (coarse mixes, extruded feeds, pellets). The main energy straights available to feed are the cereals.

TYPES OF CEREAL

> Cereals are seeds known as monocotyledons and include oats, barley, maize and wheat.

Cereal grains are essentially carbohydrate concentrates, the main component being starch, which is concentrated in the endosperm. All cereals contain low levels of calcium and high levels of phosphorus and are also low in lysine (an essential amino acid). Cereals are available whole, rolled, micronized, or extruded. Remember, however, that while cereals are often a vital part of our horse's rations, they are not a natural feed for his digestive system, so they have to be fed with care.

Whole cereals

These are an ideal way of feeding horses as long as they have good teeth. All cereals can be fed whole, but barley and wheat need soaking or cooking in hot water first to soften the cereal coat.

Rolled cereals

These are cereals that have had the husk removed and have then been crushed. Once the grain is exposed to air, however, cereals will lose their nutritional value after two weeks. Do check with your feed merchant just how long he has had the rolled oats in his store.

Micronized cereals

These are flaked and 'toasted' in equipment similar to microwaves. Because the cereal is cooked, some of the long starch molecules are

Micronized cereals look like corn flakes or muesli. Extruded cereals often look a little like dog food.

broken up, so that the horse can digest the starch more easily. The flakes are also lighter and have a bigger surface area compared to whole grains, so the horse takes longer to eat them.

Extruded cereals

These are cooked at great pressure much in the same way as pop-corn. Cereals which extrude best are those low in fibre and high in oil. Extrusion breaks up the starch molecules, and the extruded cereals weigh less than pelleted cereals so the horse takes longer to eat them.

OATS

This is the most common ingredient used throughout the world in horse feed. Oats are also the 'safest' bet if you are unsure what to feed as they are high in fibre and low in energy, and are therefore less likely to harm the horse if fed incorrectly. The actual feed value depends on the amount of husk, which will reduce the feed value and can vary from 23–35 per cent of the oat grain!

Oats are sometimes considered to have a fizzy effect on horses

> Oats are the lowest in energy out of all the cereals – lower than wheat, barley and maize.

Oats are used as a horse feed throughout the world.

and ponies, but no scientific study has been done on this unusual effect. Before you blame the oats if your horse seems fizzy, check that is not a case of you simply giving your horse more energy than he needs! Some researchers presented a new line of thought at an international conference in Germany, claiming that the starch (energy) in oats is released about two hours after digestion, which is normally about the time we ride the horse!

Naked oats

There is another type of oat known as the naked oat, which is 27 per cent higher in energy than ordinary oats. This oat has no husk, so is low in fibre and high in energy. Naked oats weigh more than the same volume of ordinary oats as they are high in oil.

Naked oats do not seem to give horses the same fizzy effect as ordinary oats. This may be because they are high in oil, which releases energy slowly; also, because they are high in energy people actually weigh how much they are feeding and are more careful about over-feeding!

Feeding oats

You can feed oats whole, as long as your horse is not very young or very old (they need to have good teeth). Feeding them whole is a good idea because they will be less dusty and all the goodness will still be in them. Rolling oats breaks open the husk and grain exposing the grain to oxygen, which means that the grain will start to deteriorate and lose feed value.

People are often cynical about feeding whole oats because they say that the horse does not digest them but passes them out whole in the droppings – this is clearly visible! If people looked closely they would see that it is only the husk (the undigestible fibre) that has passed through and that the grain itself has been digested. However if the horse is bolting his oats and not chewing properly, then it is possible that some may pass through.

Remember if you feed the traditional 'hay and oat' diet, your horse will be very deficient in calcium and probably protein. This diet needs supplementing. You can use:

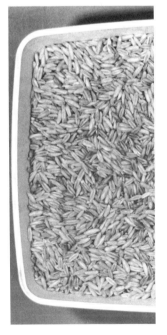

Oats without their coats.

- alfalfa   low in energy
                        high in calcium
                        high in protein

- Sugar beet — high in calcium
  low in protein
  relatively high in energy
- Specific oat balancers — high in vitamins and minerals
  relatively high in protein
  relatively high in energy

Alternatively, add a general vitamin/mineral/protein supplement to the ration.

BARLEY

Barley is quite a small grain with a hard hull (outer coat). This means that the horse cannot get it between his teeth in order to crack open the grain. The outer hull therefore needs softening or cracking before it can be fed. The simplest way to do this is to pour on boiling water an hour before feeding.

Boiled barley

Some people like to feed some warm barley to the horses in the winter. If you do it should be fed daily. Make sure you know the weight you are feeding before adding the water. Bear in mind that warm feeds do not actually increase the horse's body temperature.

Method The barley needs to be covered by water, brought to the boil and boiled until the grain is soft. A deep saucepan should be used if you are using the kitchen stove. Be careful that the barley does not boil over or boil dry – it makes a real mess of the saucepan and cooker and the kitchen will smell of a brewery! Using a slow-cooker reduces the mess on a cooker. Put 1kg (2lb) of whole barley in the pot, add water until the level rises by about 5cm (2in), and cook on low heat for six to eight hours to make about 3kg (6lb) of wet, 'boiled' barley. Remember that adding boiling water or heating a feed in water will destroy its vitamin content.

Barley cannot be fed whole unless the outer husk has been softened.

Micronized and extruded barley

Barley can be fed 'cooked' as micronized or extruded barley. Many extruded barleys have linseed oil added and these are often used instead of the traditional boiled barley.

It is possible to make a mash of these barleys by adding hot but not boiling water to them and leaving the mix to stand until it is cool enough to feed.

Extruded barley weighs less than whole barley on a volume for volume basis as it is less dense. The difference in weight is important: we are all still guilty of feeding by the scoop. A scoop of extruded barley (a nugget) weighs 1kg (2¼lb) while micronized flakes weigh 1.1kg (2½lb). Feeding a scoop of extruded barley does not make a horse as fizzy as feeding a scoop of micronized barley because the horse is getting less energy! He also eats the extruded barley more slowly.

WHEAT

Wheat is not commonly used as a straight for horses, because it commands a high price in the human market for bread, cakes and biscuits. This makes it rather expensive to feed to horses.

Wheat contains gluten, which possesses elasticity and forms a dough when making bread. It is this property of gluten that makes finely ground wheat unpalatable to horses, sometimes forming a pasty mass in the horse's mouth. Wheat is also very high in starch - 85 per cent of its endosperm is starch.

Wheat is generally only fed to horses as a by-product or if it has been steam-flaked. The two main wheat by-products fed to horses are wheat bran and breadcrumbs.

Bran

Bran is the outer seed coat and husk of the wheat and has a similar energy level to low-quality oats.

Bran is high in protein (although this is not very accessible for the horse), fibre and phosphorus and low in calcium. The phosphorus in bran can also prevent calcium in other feeds being digested properly by the horse.

Being high in fibre, bran can absorb lots of water and act as a laxative. This has a partial wiping-out effect on the bacteria in the lower gut, which can then take ten to fourteen days to repopulate.

Bran is higher in protein than oats and barley.

Wheat is used in feeds but not often as a straight.

Bran mash

Bran was used extensively once a week as bran mash for horses on a rest day. A bran mash can be likened to a human eating four bowls of a bran cereal for breakfast or a whole bowl of bran and hot water for supper!

Bran mashes should be used in the first twenty-four hours of a laminitis attack, to clear all the bad bacteria out of the gut. They can be useful for treating colic, but speak to your vet first. For wounds or swellings, bran mash makes an excellent poultice.

Recipe Bran mashes can be made by pouring boiling water on to the bran to make a thick gruel-like mix that is neither too watery nor too sloppy. Cover the black bucket with a towel or piece of hessian sack and let it 'cook' until it is cool enough to leave your finger in the gruel. Chopped carrots, apples and 50g (2oz) of salt may be added.

> Because manufacturing procedures have improved so much, bran is now very much a by-product.

Breadcrumbs

These have all the feed value of wheat (bread) but have been dried at a high temperature to reduce the moisture content down to 6 per cent. The high temperature may also break down some of the starch. Obviously, like all cereals (grains) the meal is low in calcium, and this is why manufacturers recommend feeding sugar beet and a general vitamin and mineral supplement with the product. It is high in both energy and protein.

This is Baileys' original product. Baileys recommend feeding fibre, vitamins and minerals with this high-energy, high-protein product.

MAIZE

Maize is known in the USA as corn and we eat it every morning as corn flakes! Maize is lower in fibre but higher in energy than oats: a volume of maize will give your horse twice the energy of the same volume of oats. This makes it a useful energy source for picky eaters as only a small volume needs to be fed for the horse to obtain quite a lot of energy. It can be fed cracked or micronized.

Many people think of maize as a pig feed; however, it is very suitable for feeding to horses as long as its high energy value is appreciated. Most horses in the USA are fed corn and it balances alfalfa very well.

> Maize is higher in energy than wheat, barley and oats.

> Maize is low in protein compared to the other cereal/grains. It is a useful energy source for old horses with liver problems or horses with jaundice.

Linseed is still fed by the Household Cavalry.

LINSEED

Linseed is not a cereal – it is a vegetable protein source and is the seed of the flax plant. It is high in oil (30 per cent) and protein (20 per cent). It is unique because it contains 30–100g/kg of mucilage, which forms a lovely jelly when the seeds are cooked.

It is not as popular as it used to be, probably because of the extreme mess it makes of cookers if it boils over. It also has to compete on the cooker with human dinners! This is one of the reasons that boiled barley in the bag with linseed has proved so popular.

Horses seem to do well on a small quantity of linseed; this could be because the jelly helps lubricate the feed and protects the gut wall from mechanical damage. It may also prevent constipation without being too much of a laxative and may help the horse stay 'regular'!

How to cook

You can feed 85g (3oz) a day to horses. Put the seeds directly into boiling water and then simmer for four to six hours. Plenty of water is needed, as this is what forms the jelly. Be warned, though: linseed burns and boils over very easily, so you may need to top up the water! Once cold, add the seeds and jelly to the feed with which they are being mixed.

SUGAR BEET

This is a root from the same family as the potato, and looks like a cross between a turnip and beetroot. The sugar beet is taken to the factory, sliced and soaked in water. Most of the sugar is removed and what is left is mainly fibre and pulp. This pulp is dried and then sold either as sugar beet pellets or as shreds.

Sugar beet has a similar energy content to low-quality oats, but the energy comes from digestible fibre and sucrose and *not* from starch. It can be used as the sole energy source for horses in light work when mixed with alfalfa or similar fibre feeds.

Store sugar beet pellets in a clearly marked dustbin or container so that no one will confuse them with compound pellets. Tape a warning on the lid. To prepare, soak them in twice their weight of water for twenty-four hours.

Scrub out buckets daily before resoaking sugar beet.

Sugar beet ferments easily in hot weather; do not mix fermented sugar beet with other feed as it will put the horse off its feed. Make sure you scrub sugar beet buckets out daily (before soaking another batch) to avoid contamination or fermentation.

Sugar beet *shreds*, however, do not need soaking, although most people believe they do! In the USA they are fed as a forage instead of hay to racehorses with COPD. It is probably advisable to limit your horse to 0.5kg (1lb) of unsoaked shreds in each feed.

The difference between sugar beet shreds and sugar beet pellets is similar to the difference between chaff and fibre pellets. The fibre in both types of pellet is ground to a powder and therefore the horse can chew it quickly; he may choke and the pellet may swell in his throat. He has to take much longer to chew the shreds with their longer fibre.

Sugar beet is ideal for endurance horses, hunters or any horse that sweats easily and as a feed in hot weather. It is high in pectin and will act as a reservoir for water in the horse's lower gut because it attracts and holds water molecules. Also, because it is a fibre, it provides slow-releasing energy – ideal for horses in long-distance work, and for horses that react to instant energy sources, and as a warming feed in the winter.

OIL AND FAT

> Feeding fat/oil will only make a horse fat if he is receiving more energy than he is using. Any feed fed excess to requirement will cause weight gain.

Oil is an excellent energy source for the horse. It releases energy slowly and contains no starch and no protein! The horse does not have a gall bladder and continually secretes bile to digest the fat, this takes place in the small intestine. Fat can be used to replace some of the energy that comes traditionally from cereal (starch).

Most research work on feeding fats to horses has been carried out using soya oil and other vegetable oils. Animal fat (tallow) is a cheaper form of fat but appears to be less digestible than vegetable fat.

You can buy oil from the supermarket but various manufacturers also sell it, and it is generally more cost-effective to buy from them. You literally just pour it on to the feed: two tablespoons a day will put a good gleam on your horse's coat. It can also be used as a major energy source, particularly for horses who react to fast releasing energy sources.

It is a useful energy source for fussy feeders who will only eat small quantities of feed; using fat will decrease the bulk you need to feed. Look out also for feeds that contain reasonable levels of oil such as extruded feeds, naked oats and some coarse mixes.

Fats are also extremely useful for feeding to endurance horses a they appear to increase their stamina. If fat is fed as horses start to get fit, then their metabolism will adapt to use fatty acids as an energy source, sparing glycogen/glucose for use later. It also appears that racehorses fed oil recover more quickly after races.

> Oil is one of the most cost-effective means of feeding energy to horses.

Feeding fat as an energy source to laminitics once they are back in work reduces the possibility of over-loading the large intestine with soluble starch, as less starch will be needed in the ration.

The horse has become in the last twenty years a pleasure rather than a working animal. Owners generally have to work to keep their horses rather than work with the horses, and time is always short! Many of us are new to horses and are unfamiliar with the feeding of straights.

Many stud hands swear that there is no substitute for years of experience and knowledge of feeding different horses. In the agricultural world, farmers using straights will usually use a nutritionist and a computer to formulate a 'complete' feed from these straights by taking into account the protein, fibre, oil, vitamin, mineral and energy content of *each* ingredient; how much one ingredient will dilute the effectiveness of another; what forage is being fed, and the animal's weight. How many horse feeders bother to do this?

Luckily feed firms can do the above for you and 'package' the straights into compound feeds. The ingredients used in compounds are generally a mixture of the straights already discussed but will include in addition products like peas, beans, locust bean, soya and linseed. Also included are ingredients such as oat and wheat middlings and cereal fibre meal, which are the fibrous by-products of cereals. Obviously the mixes will reflect the nutritional characteristics of the raw materials.

'Cool' mixes, for instance, can contain high levels of maize and look pretty, but will probably be high in energy as maize is higher in energy than oats and barley!

Do not feed compound feeds designed for cattle, pigs or sheep to horses. Many of these will have growth promoters in them, which can be harmful to horses.

Compound feeds have an advantage over straights in that all the guesswork and formulation has been done by the feed manufacturer, who will have analysed all his raw ingredients: what you read on the label is what your horse is getting. Most feed companies will let you have a detailed analysis on request and all reputable firms employ at least one equine nutritionist, whose job it is to help with any queries on nutrition. So if your horse has feeding problems, try phoning the manufacturer. Most nutritionists are extremely helpful and no problem is too small!

One of the main criticisms of compounds from the 'traditional' feeder is that they make it hard to vary the diet of horses on the yard, which, traditionalists claim, is necessary as every horse is different. This is true up to a point, but every horse has basically the same digestive system and a similar need for vitamins, minerals and energy (dependent on size and work load). Furthermore, compound

Check your compounder can analyse raw materials *on site* before he accepts them for using in your horse's rations.

NIR (near infra red) equipment is used for on-the-spot analysis.

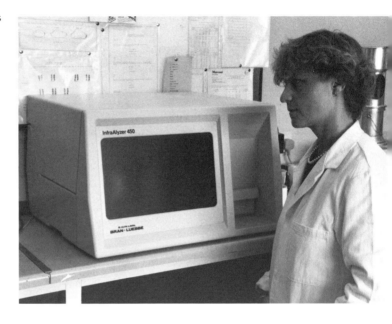

feeds do allow for variation in horses; in fact some people complain there are too many on the market!

Compounds range from low-energy horse and pony nuts, pasture nuts, pasture mix and meadow-sweet type feeds through to racing diets, performance mix, country cubes and the more specialized stud mixes, developer rations, foal creeps and oat balancers.

HOW TO READ A LABEL

The manufacturer is obliged by law to declare the protein, fibre, oil ash, vitamins A, D and E and copper content in feed. He does not have to declare energy levels, although these are actually more relevant to feeding horses than protein levels. There are very few firms who have actually scientifically established the correct energy levels of their mixes.

It is also obligatory for manufacturers to list the ingredients in descending order of amounts used. Some manufacturers use group names to 'hide' what is in their feeds.

Watch out for 'sell by' dates. Legally, manufacturers have to put 'best before' and 'use by' dates on a feed and this will be when the vitamin/mineral supplement loses its effectiveness.

If you are unsure of an ingredient then phone and ask what it is and why it is in the feed!

Good Feed is Expensive
- Good-quality, wholesome ingredients are expensive.
- Accurate weighing, mixing and manufacturing equipment is expensive.
- Analytical equipment is expensive.
- Nutritionists and other *skilled* labour have to be paid.
- Quality feeds are worth paying for; although poor quality feeds are much easier and less costly to make so you will not need to pay as much for them.

PELLETS

Pellets are made by grinding the ingredients to a powder, mixing in a little molasses to bind them together and pushing the powder through a 'dye' so that a pencil shape is formed. The pressure that is created by pushing the powder through the machine forms it into a pellet.

Pelleted feeds have various advantages:

Pelleted feeds are uniform and consistent.

1. They prevent horses from being able to leave particular ingredients they may not like.
2. The ingredients are mixed together evenly, ensuring a uniform diet.
3. They are consistent, so you always feed the same amount of everything.
4. If they are made properly there is little dust.
5. They are not as bulky as coarse mixes so require less storage space.
6. They are less expensive to make and are therefore generally cheaper than coarse mixes.
7. Because they are denser, less volume is required when compared to straights or coarse mixes – this maybe useful if you are restricting bulk intake, in the last three months of pregnancy, for example.

The disadvantages include:

1. Pellets require less chewing than coarse mixes. Since horses only produce saliva when they are physically chewing, choking is

---

Dampened pellets are useful for feeding to old horses who are unable to chew very well, as the ingredients are already ground.

more likely to occur with pellets as there is less lubrication. Feeding chaff with pellets will stop them being bolted and will overcome the risk of choking.

2. You do not know exactly what is in the pellets unless you read the label carefully or check with the manufacturer.

One scoop of coarse mix weighs 1kg (2lb); one scoop of pellets weighs 1.8kg (3lb). Weigh your feeds precisely rather than feeding by the scoop to make sure you are feeding the right amount.

COARSE MIXES

You can see what there is in a coarse mix.

These are the horse's equivalent to human muesli, and because most of us feed our horses what we think we would like to eat ourselves, coarse mixes have gained in popularity.

Coarse mixes are generally a mixture of micronized (flaked) and rolled cereals, peas and beans, and include a small pellet which usually contains the vitamins and minerals. Molasses or syrup is added in order to stop the mix becoming dusty and to stop the ingredients separating.

Advantages

1. Micronizing partially 'digests' the starch in the cereals so that the horse can digest the starch more easily himself; this way less undigested starch reaches the lower gut.
2. Horses take longer to chew coarse mixes than pellets, so more saliva is produced and food enters the stomach more slowly.
3. Fussy eaters often prefer coarse mixes.
4. It is possible to identify the ingredients used in a coarse mix by simply looking at it.
5. It is easier to put higher levels of oil in a coarse mix than in pellets, and oil is a good energy source.

Storing cereal feeds

The most important thing to consider when storing feed is how to prevent the mice and birds from eating it. You can store feed in plastic dustbins (although some persistent mice will chew these), metal dustbins or old chest freezers. The bins can be placed on pallets to improve ventilation and should be kept in a cool building

It is a good idea to label bins and bin lids with the feed that is in them. You can always cut and paste the empty bag name on to the bins. This will ensure that if for any reason you cannot feed in person, the risk of other people feeding the wrong thing is minimized. This, together with a list of horses and how much they are fed on a 'wipe clean' board, should cover all emergencies!

Supplements should be stored on a shelf or table off the floor and should be clearly marked with the name of the horse that needs the supplement. Ensure that the lids are resealed properly every time they are used, otherwise the vitamins may deteriorate.

How to feed energy feeds

The golden rule is 'little and often'. Two small feeds are of much more benefit than one large feed.

Dustbins are ideal for storing feed away from mice.

- Mix cereals with chaff to 'dilute' the effect of the cereals through the gut and to aid chewing and digestion.
- Keep to regular times: horses have internal clocks.
- Refresh your memory on the rules of feeding.
- Carrots and succulents will tempt shy eaters and help slow down greedy ones.
- A big boulder in a feed bucket will also slow down a horse's eating as he cannot then eat so easily. Make sure the horse cannot throw the boulder out.
- Let your horse have some hay first as this will take the edge off his appetite and hopefully stop him bolting his food.

Scoops come in a variety of sizes, so do weigh your feeds to be sure of the amount.

CONTAINERS

Black buckets

These should be stood in rubber tyres or placed in appropriate holders, and should have their handles removed.

Horses often throw food out of buckets in frustration, so some wastage may occur.

'Black' buckets come in a variety of colours!

You can buy matching mangers too!

Deep corner mangers

These are ideal, as long as your horse is not the nosy type who would rather be looking over the door! The large volume of these mangers allows a good weight of chaff to be fed. Some people like chest-height mangers as they feel it helps horses flex at the poll and develop neck muscles!

Mangers over the door

These are ideal for horses who just have to see what is happening! If you have a horse who is inclined to kick out because you just do not get the food to him quickly enough, this method saves you entering the stable.

Containers on the floor

These are fine if they are properly secured, have no sharp edges and will hold a reasonable volume; they also allow the horse to eat in a natural position.

All containers should be numbered or identified by colour, so each horse has his own set. They should be washed out daily to prevent stale food accumulating in corners and perhaps putting the horse off his feed. They should also be inspected for holes, dents and sharp edges.

OTHER USEFUL EQUIPMENT

- Hang a scrubbing brush on your water tap and use it for cleaning water and feed containers.
- A broom and dustpan and brush should be kept in the feed room for sweeping up any spilt feed.
- A bin in the feed room (even if it is only an empty sack) should be provided for waste sacks, paper, bits of string and sweepings off the floor.
- A set of scales is useful.
- A note pad and secure pen is also very useful for leaving messages.
- Remember not to run out of feed, but at the same time ensure that you do not put new feed on top of old feed in storage bins.

An ideal way to feed horses outside.

Freeze-marking horses is an effective theft deterrent.

Horses are herd animals that enjoy roaming. All horses should be turned out daily for as long as is practically possible. Keeping a horse in a stable for twenty-two out of twenty-four hours is similar to shutting ourselves in a classroom or the office all day and all night, day in, day out, for months on end: we'd have behavioural problems when we were let out!

Grass is a major part of the horse's environment and you should spend as much time looking after the pasture as you do on any other aspect of horse management. The most fortunate horses will obtain up to 75 per cent of their nutrition from grass.

FENCING

There are a number of ways to fence a paddock. Ideal fencing is the post and rail type, but it must be maintained properly. It is also necessary to treat the top rail with creosote to prevent horses from chewing it.

Another good method is hedging, which has the added benefit of providing a source of shelter and shade, but you must check for poisonous plants. Hedges will need maintaining to ensure they are horse-proof and fencing within the hedge may be necessary.

Electric fencing is useful for dividing fields, but not for external fencing.

Posts and wire are another form of fencing, cheaper than post and rail, but it may be advisable to have the top strand barbed. There is the risk that the wire may work loose, so it should be checked regularly.

Combination fence of post, rail, and wire. Chewing of the top bar can be discouraged with the application of a proprietary product designed for the purpose.

Sheep fencing is far from ideal, and is really not suitable for horse paddocks since horses are inclined to put a foot through the wire and get it caught. Similarly, a fence with more than one strand of barbed wire is dangerous because horses are inquisitive creatures and are likely to put a head or foot through wire, causing damage to themselves.

Gates

The five-bar gate and those with sliding posts are both common and serviceable, but padlock them!

Post and rail fencing.

Hedges can provide an ideal enclosure, but may be less horse-proof in winter!

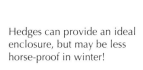

Sheep fencing can be dangerous.

Barbed wire can be very dangerous when used to fence fields for horses.

Shelter must be provided. Note the wide exit and entrance to these shelters at Redwings Horse Sanctuary.

SHELTER

A horse at grass must be provided with shelter, which must be adequate to give protection from rain and wind in the winter, and from the sun and flies in the summer.

Hedges and trees are good for shelter, but the leaves fall off in winter, which may reduce effectiveness. A purpose-built field shelter is ideal, but it should be positioned with its back to the prevailing wind, and it should have a wide opening to stop bullying.

PASTURE MAINTENANCE

Good maintenance is extremely important if a horse is to make good use of pasture. Weeds should be kept under control: pull up nettles, thistles, docks, buttercups, foxgloves, chickweed, and moss.

It is still more important to check for poisonous plants, such as ragwort, which damages the liver (horses will eat ragwort when dried, so check hay). Yew, which affects the heart, is also poisonous and should be removed, as should laburnum, deadly nightshade, and bracken.

ACREAGE

Ideally, there should be 1½–4 acres (½–1½ hectares) of grass per

WEEDS

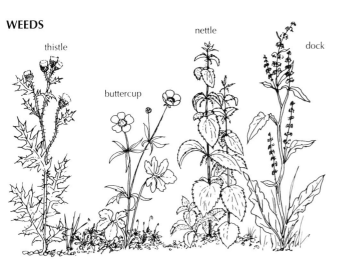

thistle nettle dock buttercup

If your field is growing weeds, there is less grass available. Pull up weeds and poisonous plants.

POISONOUS PLANTS

yew laburnum

deadly nightshade foxglove ragwort

Learn to recognize poisonous plants. It is worth buying a well-illustrated field reference book and taking it with you when you check your field.

horse. This allows you to fence off and rest part of the field/paddock.

TYPES OF GRASS

The type of grass you wish to see in your paddock will depend upon whether you want to divide some of the land for hay making. Good grasses are: ryegrass, fescue, meadow grass and timothy. White clover is useful but be careful as it can suffocate grass especially during drought, and its growth can be very dificult to control.

FERTILIZERS AND WEED KILLERS

There are specific chemicals designed for use on horse pasture, so do use these rather than any other product, as the fertilizers are generally lower in nitrogen compared to those used on dairy or recreational areas. If in doubt ask your local ADAS office or speak to a specialist fertilizer company.

You may need to harrow and roll your fields after fertilizing or reseeding.

WORM CONTROL

This is extremely important as pasture forms part of the worms' life-cycle. In order to reduce the risk of worm infestation, pick up droppings regularly, rest your fields, and do not overgraze.

Ideally, rotate your grazing – see if you can borrow sheep or cows.

Worming programme

However well your pasture is managed, it will still be necessary to worm your horse. At pasture, your horse can pick up bots, roundworms, threadworms, tapeworms, lungworms, redworms, whiteworms, and pinworms.

Speak to your vet for advice on an effective worming programme

As if by instinct horses do avoid grazing too close to 'roughs (clumps of droppings). Up to 50 per cent of grazing area can be los

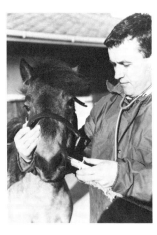

Horses should be wormed regularly; if there is a group of horses, they should all be wormed at the same time.

Droppings are the main source of worms, so if they are picked up regularly worm control is much more effective.

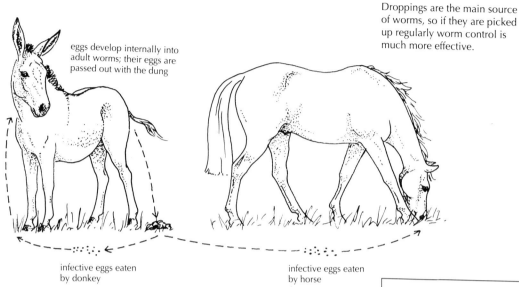

eggs develop internally into adult worms; their eggs are passed out with the dung

infective eggs eaten by donkey

infective eggs eaten by horse

Very hot or very cold (frosty) weather will kill larvae and expose eggs. Make sure grass is very short in the roughs so larvae can be exposed. Ten to twelve weeks' exposure to cold, frosty weather will kill the larvae.

to roughs and these areas can have up to fifteen times the worm contamination of the short-grazed grass ('lawns').

If you harrow the roughs to break up the manure, do not spread the droppings on to the uncontaminated part of the field.

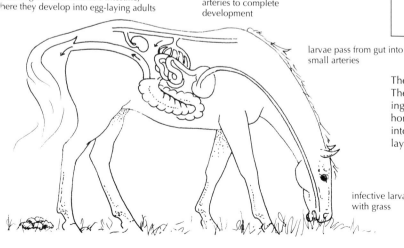

larvae migrate to the horse's intestine, where they develop into egg-laying adults

larvae move to main arteries to complete development

larvae pass from gut into small arteries

The life cycle of the lungworm. The life cycle is halted after ingestion by a horse as, in horses, few eggs will develop into adult worms capable of laying eggs.

infective larvae eaten with grass

GENERAL MAINTENANCE

Good-quality pasture will provide a healthy, mature horse in light work with a balanced, healthy diet (providing the paddock is not over-stocked), from spring until late autumn.

Grass should not be allowed to become excessively tall or mature. Tall grass is generally not eaten, but trampled as the horse searches for the more palatable parts. Mature grass, particularly as it dries off, becomes less nutritious.

Italian ryegrass   Perennial ryegrass

Cock's-foot

Species	Italian Ryegrass	Perennial Ryegrass	Cocksfoot
Land needed	Most soil types	God land Good feeding	Dry conditions
Time grown for	Grown for one or two leys	Permanent grassland and leys	In leys
Usage	Quick growing, high yielding, good seed crop, grazing and cutting	Good for grazing, cutting, last long time on good land	Strong, deep rooted, produces lot of growth but not as palatable
Maximum growth period	Early spring growth	Early spring and summer but is hard wearing and stays green in winter	During summer when Ryegrass doesn't produce so much
Leaf	Dull and ribbed on top. Glossy underneath	As Italian	Light green, rough edges
Base stem	Red	Red	Light
Texture	Smooth	Smooth	Rough
How it grows	Tufted	Tufted	Tufted

If your paddock is small then you can use a strimmer to cut the grass (wear protective clothing and watch out for nettles!). Fresh, growing grasses are more palatable, so remove the long, cut grass.

If you have a large area then get the long grass baled by a friendly farmer who can use it for feeding cattle, sheep or goats. Alternatively, and ideally, move the horses out after you have wormed them and graze off the grass with sheep or cattle. However, grass should not be grazed too short as this will increase the uptake of worms, teeth problems and risk of sand colic on sandy soils.

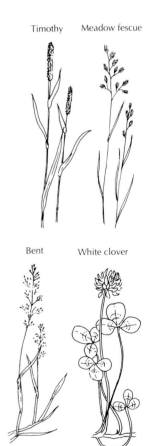

Timothy   Meadow fescue

Bent   White clover

Timothy	Meadow Fescue	Bent	White Clover
Good land; does not compete well with Cocksfoot	Very similar to Timothy	Very common	In permanent grasslands unless short of lime, well drained
In mixture with fescue	Very similar to Timothy	Permanent grassland	Often sown in April
Very palatable grazing and cropping	Very similar to Timothy	Stems run over surface to form a 'mat' hard wearing surface	Very good hay. Seed needs to be dressed with nitrogen fixing bacteria
Late spring and through summer. Stays green in winter	Early spring into autumn and stays green in winter	Late in year. Produces very little but very palatable	Late spring and summer
Light green	As Italian Ryegrass	Long and narrow	Three leaflets, pointed tips and ragged edge
Brown. Can swell	Red	Creeping	Green (flower violet, blue)
Smooth	Smooth	Smooth	Smooth
Tufted	Tufted	Stolons (like strawberries)	Tufted

The word supplement can be replaced by words such as additive, extra, re-enforcement, accessory to, complement, satisfy, complete. But just what constitutes an unbalanced diet in the first place is a tricky question, and with over 150 supplements on the market, each claiming to be the best, which one you should use, if indeed you need one at all, becomes almost impossible to decide.

Obviously horses have had their diets naturally supplemented for years. Pastures and hedgerows were full of wild herbs and 'weeds' containing minerals and vitamins and soil contains minerals, as does tree bark.

HERBS

The most 'natural' supplements available today are herbs. These have numerous properties and some of the claims made by manufacturers are medicinal ones. However, beware any herb or supplement that claims it can *cure* a problem. The manufacturers are probably not legally allowed to state this and it is probably impossible to justify the claim scientifically.

You may feel you need to supplement the feed with herbs if your horse has restricted grazing, poor-quality hay, low intakes of cereals, a poor coat or a behavioural problem. If the problem persists or if you are in any way uncertain of its cause, call the vet before treating it with herbal remedies.

Some of the more common herbs used in mixes include:

- Balm — antispasmodic, tonic, digestive
- Camomile — sedative, analgesic
- Cow parsnip — sedative, aphrodisiac, digestive
- Dandelion — laxative, tonic
- Fennel — diuretic, expectorant, antispasmodic
- Garlic — 'antibiotic', intestinal disinfectant, insect repellant
- Garlic mustard — anticatarrhal, anti-asthmatic
- Lavender — antiseptic, tonic, antispasmodic
- Peppermint — tonic, antispasmodic, insecticide
- Rosehip — laxative, diuretic, astringent
- Thyme — antiseptic, diuretic, expectorant
- Valerian — sedative, anti-epileptic, Cartiotonic, anti-depressant
- White dead-nettle — vasoconstrictive

Most herbal manufacturers admit that much of their evidence of effectiveness is descriptive rather than scientific and based on human rather than equine remedies. Some manufacturers now regularly send blood and urine samples of horses on their herbal supplements to a forensic laboratory for testing while others have started to do some work with vets. These are promising developments.

Scientific work with herbs is difficult as many of the effects are subjective observations; for example, you expect your horse to be quieter when fed placid mix, so this is what you observe.

When to use

If you know of someone for whom herbs have worked and your horse has a similar problem, then try the remedy.

Do not mix herb preparations, as some herbs will react with others, and some can be dangerous in large quantities. Buy only from reputable manufacturers, and be wary of any making large claims for 'cure-alls'!

OTHER SUPPLEMENTS

Horses in light work rarely need their diets supplementing; however, if your horse is stressed, kept stabled, fed preserved roughages, worked hard, sweats a lot, has limited access to grass or if you live in an area where there are known deficiencies then supplements may have a role to play. They may also be useful if you are feeding mares and foals and are restricting their feed or if you are feeding straights.

Common supplements

Salt All horses will benefit from 50g (2oz) of salt a day.

Cod Liver Oil This is a useful source of vitamins A, D and E, especially in the winter.

Cider Vinegar This can help to relieve the symptoms of arthritis in horses that suffer from it.

Probiotics These are a mixture of live bacteria, which producers claim helps to recolonize the horse's lower gut. We do not understand as yet what species of bacteria and what interactions there are in the lower gut; this lack of knowledge has been highlighted as a research priority.

Yeasts   Yeast has been scientifically evaluated in horses and has been proven to create a more stable lower gut environment. It increases the number of fibre-digesting bacteria in the lower gut and helps improve fibre digestion.

Yeasts are not probiotics as they do not contain live bacteria. Most horses will benefit from having yeast (*sacchromyces carivisae*[1066]) in their diets.

What to look for in a supplement

Always read the label before you buy. You need to know how much there is of each vitamin and mineral that is in your horse's daily dose. This must be stated in sensible units, not given per kilogram, as you do not feed a kilogram of supplement a day; such numbers are meaningless.

> Biotin only supplements are rarely expensive, but it appears that biotin needs calcium, methionine and zinc to be present in order to be effective.

Cost

The cost per day is a much more significant figure than the cost per tub.

Vitamins A and D are cheap to include, as is calcium. Vitamin E, however, is expensive, as is phosphorus.

Quantities

Some supplements contain fewer vitamins and minerals than compound feeds, so check what is in a kilogram of supplement compared to a kilo of compound feed. It may prove much more cost-effective simply to feed compounds.

SCIENCE

This is still a relatively new area of equine nutrition, and there are still many grey areas in scientists' knowledge. Because of this it is important not to take everything a manufacturer claims at face value. If a manufacturer is unable to justify the claims he makes for his product scientifically, or if he is reluctant or unable to answer your questions, do not buy from him; an ethical manufacturer will not mind you asking questions.

LAMINITIS

Having discussed how to feed and what feeds are available, it is also necessary to understand what can go wrong if we mismanage our horses. It must be appreciated that by domesticating our horses we have changed their natural environment, so problems may quite easily arise even if on the surface we appear to be doing everything correctly, and laminitis, which is often caused by nutritional imbalance 'is one of the most common causes of lameness and disability of horses and ponies in this country' according to Robert Eustace of the Laminitis Clinic.

What is Laminitis?

Laminitis is a disease of the foot that results from an interruption of normal blood flow to the foot; it is a little like the foot having a stroke so that structures within it become damaged.

The laminae in the horse's foot are damaged first. These hold together the pedal bone and the outside hoof capsule. The pedal bones supports the whole weight of the horse. If the laminae start to degenerate then the pedal bone is no longer held in the correct position and will start to drop.

All four feet can be affected but often it is just the front feet. Initially the horse or pony may just seem to be uncomfortable, constantly shifting weight from one foot to another; remember a horse does not normally fidget in the front, so take any signs of this seriously. The horse may not want to walk or trot and will be in so much pain that he will often just lie down. Other signs include a pounding digital pulse and warm feet.

In severe cases (or if you do not act quickly), the pedal bone can sink or rotate through the sole of the foot within twenty-four hours. Usually, if this happens, the horse would have to be destroyed. If the horse is lucky the laminae will heal and rebind the hoof wall and the pedal bone, but the foot will never be the same as it was before the attack.

Causes

Laminitis is not caused by poor diet alone; there are a number of other possibilities.

Obesity or overeating   This is the most common cause in the UK.

Laminitis should always be regarded as an emergency and a vet and farrier called.

The stance typically adopted by the laminitic horse.

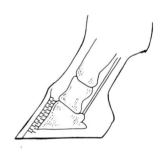

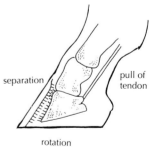

separation   pull of tendon

rotation

Comparison of a normal and laminitic foot, showing rotation of the pedal bone.

Unfortunately, animals that are overweight (that is, in show condition) are more prone to laminitis and even a slight decrease in exercise or a slight increase in feed can tip the balance.

Native ponies require very little to eat. Remember that they evolved to manage (and manage very well at that) on sparse scrubland and mountain grazing, not rich grass pastures. Large meals of cereals can also trigger laminitis.

Toxaemia (poisoning) Anything that causes the horse to become systemically ill (that is, that causes toxins to circulate in the blood), for example diarrhoea, pneumonia, retention of afterbirth and colic, can lead to laminitis.

Drugs An attack can sometimes occur after worming or vaccination. Corticosteroid treatment also often triggers laminitis.

Hormones Pituitary tumours can result in Cushings disease, which can lead on to laminitis; this condition usually affects older horses (*see* Cushings Disease).

Mechanical causes Any traumatic pounding of the feet can cause constriction of the blood vessels in the foot. Driving ponies often get this type of laminitis, but any horse that is trotted frequently on hard surfaces could be a victim.

What goes wrong?

Laminitis is caused by overloading the digestive system or stressing the system in some way, which alters the microbial population in the hind gut.

The horse evolved to eat eighteen out of twenty-four hours; that is, eat little and often. Consequently, their stomachs are very small and can be over-loaded very easily. If the stomach is over-loaded, it pushes the food through the small intestine very quickly. The horse's enzymes do not have time to digest all the food properly and some will reach the large intestine undigested.

Soluble carbohydrates (starch) should all be digested in the small intestine; a trickle of undigested starch reaching the large intestine is fine, but if a large quantity suddenly passes through then real problems start.

Once in the large intestine the starch acts as an 'instant' energy source rather like a chocolate bar; it is broken down very quickly

> Overfeeding of protein does not cause laminitis; it is overfeeding of soluble carbohydrates (starch) that is the main dietary cause.

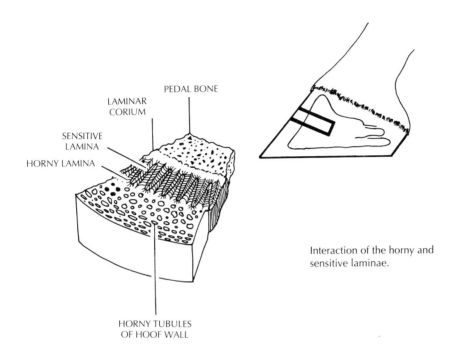

PEDAL BONE

LAMINAR
CORIUM

SENSITIVE
LAMINA

HORNY LAMINA

HORNY TUBULES
OF HOOF WALL

Interaction of the horny and
sensitive laminae.

and easily and the bacteria breaking down the chocolate bar grow very quickly. However, the fibre-digesting bacteria have to break into the fibre before they can release the nutrients within it and they grow slowly.

As the chocolate bar bacteria digest the starch, they produce by-products known as volatile fatty acids and lactic acid. These create an acid gut. If the problem stops here the horse may merely suffer from indigestion (mild colic). However, the fibre-digesting bacteria cannot survive the acid conditions and start to die. As they die, their cell walls rupture and endotoxins (poisons) are released; this makes the stomach ache considerably worse.

The acid conditions damage the gut wall, allowing the poison to seep out of the gut and into the bloodstream. The lactic acid can also be passively absorbed into the bloodstream creating acid conditions (acidosis) throughout the body. Once the poisons get into the bloodstream, a reaction happens during which hormones are released, one of which is histamine. Histamine affects the blood supply, causing blood to be taken away from the feet – and this is the start of laminitis.

Immediate treatment

1. Call the vet and farrier immediately.
2. Remove your horse from whatever is causing the acid conditions (for example, lush grass), because if acidosis continues the whole system becomes poisoned and the horse may die.
3. Feed bran mash for twenty-four hours to remove toxins; do this under the vet's supervision.
4. Do not do anything that will put your horse in any more pain.
5. Put him on a roughage diet that is high in fibre, low in sugars and high in calcium.

Hyperlipaemia

It is *vital* that you do not starve laminitic horses. If you do the horse will break down the fat on its back to stay alive: all animals need energy to keep their hearts beating. The fat will be mobilized very quickly and the horse's metabolism will change. Lots of fatty acids are released into the bloodstream and they literally clog up the circulation. The heart cannot pump the fat round the blood and the horse keels over and dies.

Restrict your horse's grazing; sometimes the only grass he can have is on the end of a lead rope.

Control and prevention

Follow the guidelines below for a horse recovering from laminitis (or for one at risk) to ensure it does not happen again.

- Feed bulk roughage with a low feed value, such as oat straw.
- Reduce hay and bulk out with straw.
- Feed fibrous feeds when the horse is back in work, not cereals; use Hi-Fi, Alfa-A, pasture nuts or high fibre cubes.
- Keep him on 'bare' paddocks.
- Turn out on sand arenas for some of the time.
- Use a muzzle for some of the time.
- Use electric fencing to restrict access to grass.
- Beg, borrow or buy sheep or cattle to keep the grass down.
- Increase work load before increasing feed.
- Feed little and often, so you do not overload the stomach.
- Do *not* overfeed.

CUSHINGS DISEASE

If your horse is elderly and seems to have a winter coat all year round, watch out for the following signs:

- Drinking excess water
- Frequent urinating
- Sweating easily
- Pot belly but thin around the hips
- Susceptibility to laminitis.

If he has these symptoms, he may have a problem with his pituitary gland and it is worth having a chat to your vet.

Dietary needs for a pony with Cushings disease

If your pony is diagnosed as having Cushings disease, you should feed him, every day, 50g (2oz) of salt, sugar beet, soya oil and as much hay and alfalfa as he likes. You could also include cereals in his feed if he is not susceptible to laminitis.

COLIC

Colic is stomach ache or indigestion. There are several types of cause, and not all of them are related to feeding. Those that are, are impactation and gas colic.

> If you suspect colic call the vet.

Impactation

This can occur when very woody hay is fed, when a horse is moved from grass on to hay, or from a high cereal diet to a high hay diet. The bacteria in the large colon cannot digest the food so it gets 'stuck' where the tube narrows.

Gas colic

This may be caused by the rapid fermentation of food or by the feeding of grass cuttings. Gases are produced that may get trapped along the gut, causing it to distend.

The main cause of colic is probably similar to that of laminitis – too much readily fermentable starch and not enough roughage.

Following the rules of feeding outlined in this book should prevent colic from breaking out.

Symptoms

A horse suffering from colic may:

1. Turn his head frequently to look at his flanks.
2. Sweat because he is in pain.
3. Have a disturbed bed.
4. Produce hard, small, shiny droppings, or no droppings at all.
5. Produce a lot of abdominal rumblings and noises.
6. Lose his appetite and stop eating.
7. Keep rolling.
8. Have an increased temperature.

COPD

This is chronic obstructive pulmonary disease, also known as SAD (small airway disease). The main symptoms are broken wind and coughing.

This problem is partially nutritional as the main cause is dusty hay, something that unfortunately is very common in the UK. The disease is virtually unheard of in hot, dry climates partly because horses are out more and because hay is dried properly.

COPD is caused by an allergic lung reaction to inhaled small dust particles, particularly moulds. These moulds are found in hay and straw that has not been dried properly. If a horse breathes these particles in they can cause an inflammation in the small airways (bronchioles). The walls can become thickened, mucus is produced and the muscles in the lungs can go into spasms, making it difficult for the horse to breathe.

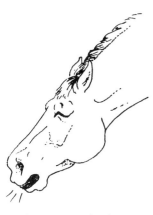

Symptoms

Cough   This is often seen at rest and is made worse with exercise. Sometimes horses may only cough after being cantered.

Runny Nose   Sometimes this is only seen when the head is at ground level or lowered. This is because many horses will swallow the mucus in their trachea and so do not get runny noses.

Coughing is unusual in horses, so if your horse coughs regularly it is important to investigate the possible causes. Veterinary assistance will usually be necessary.

Increased Breathing Rate If your horse has to make an effort to breath, he develops extra muscles, which are visible as the 'heave' line between abdomen and chest wall. If this happens, you must call the vet. Shallow, rapid breathing is a bad sign.

Cure

Remove the afflicted horse fully from contact with hay and straw, and if possible turn him out. Otherwise you will need to control bedding, stabling and forage to ensure they are dust-free.

Feed If you continue to feed hay, soak it and make sure it does not dry out. It is essential that the soaking is thorough and complete. Bear in mind that some nutrients are lost in the water.

Alternatively you can use haylage, which was described under Hay Alternatives. Do bear in mind that it is 50 per cent water, so you need to feed quite a lot to make sure your horse is getting adequate fibre. Furthermore, although the protein value is similar to that of hay, haylage is higher in energy. Horses also enjoy haylage and tend to eat it quickly, which could possibly lead to boredom problems.

Short-chop forages are designed to be fed in the same quantity as hay. Methods of feeding short-chop forages are also discussed in the Hay Alternatives section.

Bedding Use only very clean and dust-free straw. Alternatives are chopped, dust-extracted straw, hemp, shavings, paper and peat.

Beds must be managed properly because if they get damp fungal growth can occur. It is important to remove wet bedding daily.

Stabling Make sure the stable is well ventilated but not draughty. Rug a horse to keep him warm rather than putting him in a stuffy stable.

Stable him away from other horses on hay and straw, as spores can easily be blown to adjacent stables.

Some herbal remedies are available that are reputed to alleviate coughs, and you can also buy drugs that will help the condition.

TYING-UP

This problem is also known as Monday morning disease and Set-fast, and no one really knows what causes it, although cases have been recognized for over 100 years! It can be likened to severe cramp in humans and muscle damage can occur.

> There is no point removing dust from your horse's stable if horses next to him are on hay and straw, if he is kept close to the hay barn or downwind from the muck heap. Remember that dust is airborne.

> Empty containers in which you soak hay *daily*. The water in which you soak hay has a biological value ten times that of raw sewage.

Use soaked hay for horse with COPD (persistent cough).

Signs

The signs are stiffness, and a change in stride. Sometimes the horse seizes up totally and is unable to move.

Possible causes

This condition can arise if horses are fed a lot but are then not exercised. Horses that sweat a lot during exercise or that are unfit so that oxygen cannot be supplied to the muscles quickly enough, can also be affected.

Action

In general, you should always make sure that your horse is fit enough to do the job you are asking of him.

- Do not move the horse more than necessary; load him into a trailer rather than walk him if he has to be moved.
- Keep him warm.
- Call the vet.
- Reduce or cut out altogether hard feed.
- Feed electrolytes if the horse sweats a lot.

Understanding your horse's needs will help you establish a lasting partnership.

SUMMARY

Although nutrition may seem a complex subject, many of the basics are still unknown. We do not know precisely how much grass a horse eats, we do not know what types of bacteria are in his lower gut, we do not know in detail how the minerals interact.

However, we have been feeding and riding horses for thousands of years and they are not extinct yet! The most important fact to remember is that a horse is a forage eater.

Follow the rules of feeding at all times. An open mind will learn, so do ask advice if you are in doubt; fatal mistakes can be made otherwise. There are always qualified nutritionists available who will be only too pleased to help.

If you want to learn more equine nutrition, look out for lectures on feeding in your area or make the most of shows, where nutritionists are often available.

Amino Acids   These constitute a small but essential part of protein. Lots of amino acids make up one protein, rather like letters make words. Some amino acids must be in the horse's diet, others he can make for himself.

Amylase   An enzyme (a chemical) that breaks up large starch molecules into small particles that can be absorbed from the gut to the bloodstream.

Analysis   Tests done on feedstuffs to find out exactly what levels of nutrients are contained within them.

At grass   The horse is at grass when he is turned out in a field for at least 50 per cent of his time. Often the horse is kept out with shelter for twenty-four hours; such a horse will be resting or in light work.

Bile   A chemical required to digest fat.

Chaff   This is chopped forages (such as hay, straw or alfalfa). The forage is usually chopped to 12–50mm (½–2in) in length and is fed in the food bucket rather than in a hay-net. Chaff sometimes contains herbs, limestone and molasses.

Concentrates   These are feeds that are high in energy, protein and vitamins and minerals. They are designed to be fed in small quantities, unlike forage.

Digestible energy   The amount of energy the horse can obtain from his food. This is measured in MJ (mega-joules). MJs can be loosely compared to human calories.

Electrolytes   Minerals that are carried in solution in the blood These minerals contribute to the osmotic pressure of the blood They are lost in large quantities in sweat.

Equine dentist   A person who has undergone training to specialize in horses' tooth care. Usually he is more thorough than a vet, but do check qualifications.

Forage   Food that a horse would normally forage for in the wild such as grass, herbs, mature grass or hay and straw. It contains large quantities of fibre and is normally lower in feed value than concentrates.

Mash   An out-dated method of adding hot water (normally) to bran to give a gruel-like meal to a horse.

Oxidation   A chemical change, often resulting in loss of a nutrient This process needs oxygen to take place.

Roughage   *see* 'forage'. Sometimes forage of very low feed value is called roughage.

Scoop   A measuring bowl with a handle specifically designed for putting feed into a horse's bucket. You should know the exact weight of each feed that your scoop holds.

Thoroughbred The racing breed of horse developed from crossing one of three imported oriental breeds of stallion with indigenous mares. The breed has been exported all over the world.

Top line An excess of fat that show judges like to see on show animals; it gives them an exaggerated rounded appearance that judges find pleasing to the eye.

Trickle feeding Eating almost continuously. Animals that do this have very small stomachs so cannot store meals. Carnivores (meat eaters) have large stomachs and do not need to trickle feed as they can store meals in their stomachs for several days if necessary.

Weigh-bridge A large set of scales that are designed to allow a horse or a lorry to be put on them to be weighed exactly.

Weigh-tape A tape measure that has been specially calibrated so that you can find a horse's weight by measuring his heart girth. It is one of the easiest and most accurate ways of 'weighing' a horse.

FURTHER READING • 95

Eustace, R   *Explaining Laminitis and Its Prevention*

Watering and Feeding BHS   *The Manual of Stable Management* (Kenilworth Press, 1992)

Frape, D   *Equine Nutrition and Feeding* (Longman, 1986)

Launert, E   *The Hamlyn Guide to Edible and Medicinal Plants of Britain and Northern Europe* (Hamlyn)

Cheij, Roberto   *The Macdonald Encyclopedia of Medicinal Plants* (Macdonald, 1984)

Launder and Lucas   *Feeding Facts* (DJ Murphy, 1986)

McCarthy, G   *Pasture Management for Horses and Ponies* (Collins Professional Books, 1987)

van Lennep, J   *First Foal* (Allan & Co)

alfalfa, 57
automatic waterers, 17

barley, 61
bran, 62
buckets, 72

carbohydrate, 10, 47
cereals, 58
chewing, 6
cider vinegar, 83
coarse mixes, 70
cod liver oil, 83
colic, 89
condition scoring, 25
COPD, 90, 91
Cushings disease, 89

diets:
    breeding mares, 34
    cold weather, 39
    foals, 36
    old horses, 38
    ponies, 29
    poor condition, 40
    show/dressage horse, 31
    two year olds, 37
    yearlings, 37
digestive system, 8

fats, 11
feed quantities, calculating, 26
fencing, 74

grass, 47
    types of, 80, 81

hay, 49
    feeding, 51
haylage, 54
herbs, 82
high fibre pellets, 56

labels, 68
    reading, 68
laminitis, 66, 85
    treatment, 88

large intestine, 9
linseed, 64

maize, 63
mangers, 72
mould, 50
mouth, 6

oats, 59
    feeding, 60
oil (fat), 66

pellets, 69
poisonous plants, 77
probiotics, 83
problems:
    fussy feeders, 43
    nervy, 42
    overweight, 42
    poor coat, 41
    poor foot growth, 40
protein, 11, 47

roughage (fibre), 19, 32, 39, 48

saliva, 7
salt, 83
shelter, 76
small intestine, 9
stomach, 7, 9, 18
straw, 55
sugar beet, 64

troughs, 16
tying-up, 91

water, 15, 16, 17
weight:
    of feed, 21
    of horses, 22
wheat, 62
work loads, 25
worm control, 78

yeast, 84